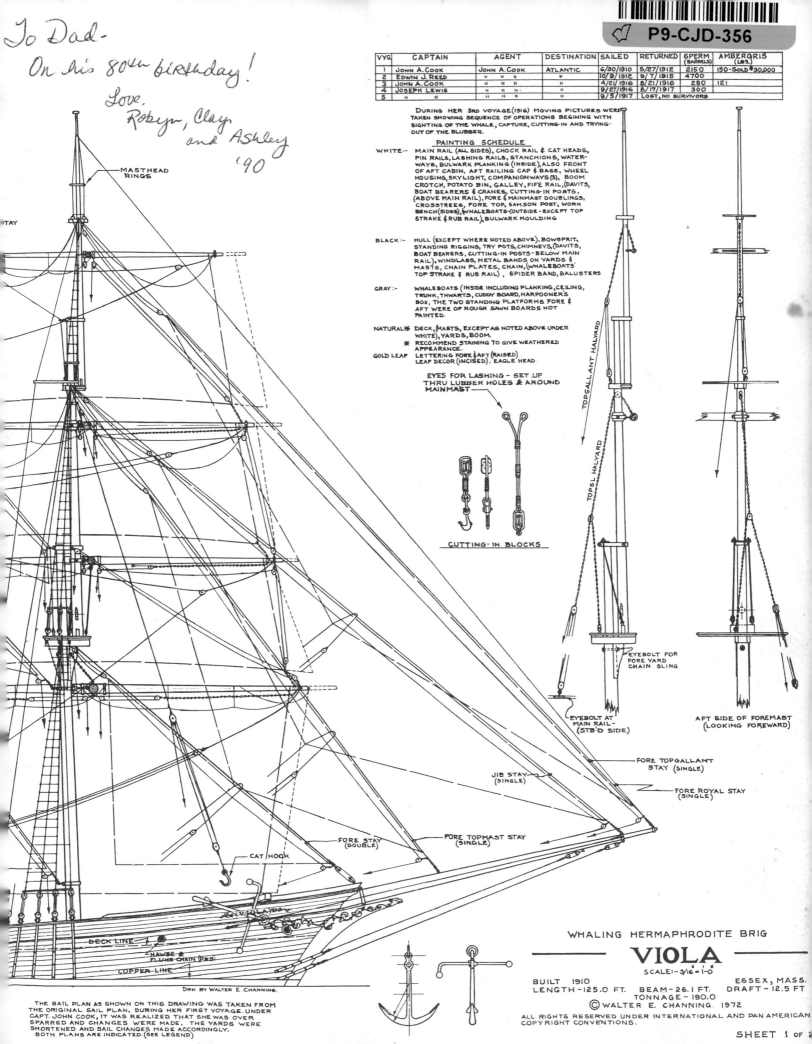

To Dad-
On his 80th birthday!
Love,
Robyn, Clay
and Ashley
'90

VYG	CAPTAIN	AGENT	DESTINATION	SAILED	RETURNED	SPERM (BARRELS)	AMBERGRIS (LBS.)
1	John A. Cook	John A. Cook	Atlantic	6/30/1910	5/27/1912	2150	150-Sold $30,000
2	Edwin J. Reed	"	"	10/9/1912	9/7/1915	4700	
3	John A. Cook	"	"	4/21/1916	8/21/1916	280	121
4	Joseph Lewis	"	"	9/27/1916	8/17/1917	300	
5				9/5/1917	Lost, no survivors		

DURING HER 3RD VOYAGE (1916) MOVING PICTURES WERE TAKEN SHOWING SEQUENCE OF OPERATIONS BEGINING WITH SIGHTING OF THE WHALE, CAPTURE, CUTTING-IN AND TRYING-OUT OF THE BLUBBER.

PAINTING SCHEDULE

WHITE:- MAIN RAIL (ALL SIDES), CHOCK RAIL & CAT HEADS, PIN RAILS, LASHING RAILS, STANCHIONS, WATER-WAYS, BULWARK PLANKING (INSIDE), ALSO FRONT OF AFT CABIN, AFT RAILING CAP & BASE, WHEEL HOUSING, SKYLIGHT, COMPANIONWAYS (3), BOOM CROTCH, POTATO BIN, GALLEY, FIFE RAIL, (DAVITS, BOAT BEARERS & CRANES, CUTTING-IN POSTS, (ABOVE MAIN RAIL), FORE & MAINMAST DOUBLINGS, CROSSTREES, FORE TOP, SAMSON POST, WORK BENCH (SIDES), (WHALEBOATS-(OUTSIDE - EXCEPT TOP STRAKE & RUB RAIL), BULWARK MOULDING.

BLACK:- HULL (EXCEPT WHERE NOTED ABOVE), BOWSPRIT, STANDING RIGGING, TRY POTS, CHIMNEYS, (DAVITS, BOAT BEARERS, CUTTING-IN POSTS - BELOW MAIN RAIL), WINDLASS, METAL BANDS ON YARDS & MASTS, CHAIN PLATES, CHAIN, (WHALEBOATS TOP STRAKE & RUB RAIL), SPIDER BAND, BALUSTERS.

GRAY:- WHALEBOATS (INSIDE INCLUDING PLANKING, CEILING, TRUNK, THWARTS, CUDDY BOARD, HARPOONER'S BOX, THE TWO STANDING PLATFORMS FORE & AFT WERE OF ROUGH SAWN BOARDS NOT PAINTED.

NATURAL* DECK, (MASTS, EXCEPT AS NOTED ABOVE UNDER WHITE), YARDS, BOOM.
* RECOMMEND STAINING TO GIVE WEATHERED APPEARANCE.

GOLD LEAF LETTERING FORE & AFT (RAISED), LEAF DECOR (INCISED), EAGLE HEAD.

EYES FOR LASHING - SET UP THRU LUBBER HOLES & AROUND MAINMAST

CUTTING-IN BLOCKS

TOPGALLANT HALYARD

TOPSL HALYARD

EYEBOLT FOR FORE YARD CHAIN SLING

EYEBOLT AT MAIN RAIL - (STB'D SIDE)

AFT SIDE OF FOREMAST (LOOKING FOREWARD)

FORE TOPGALLANT STAY (SINGLE)

FORE ROYAL STAY (SINGLE)

JIB STAY (SINGLE)

FORE STAY (DOUBLE)

FORE TOPMAST STAY (SINGLE)

CAT HOOK

MASTHEAD RINGS

STAY

DECK LINE

HAWSE & FLUKE CHAIN (P&S)

COPPER-LINE

DRN BY WALTER E. CHANNING.

THE SAIL PLAN AS SHOWN ON THIS DRAWING WAS TAKEN FROM THE ORIGINAL SAIL PLAN. DURING HER FIRST VOYAGE UNDER CAPT. JOHN COOK, IT WAS REALIZED THAT SHE WAS OVER SPARRED AND CHANGES WERE MADE. THE YARDS WERE SHORTENED AND SAIL CHANGES MADE ACCORDINGLY. BOTH PLANS ARE INDICATED. (SEE LEGEND)

WHALING HERMAPHRODITE BRIG
VIOLA
SCALE:- 3/16=1-0

BUILT 1910
LENGTH-125.0 FT. BEAM-26.1 FT. DRAFT-12.5 FT
TONNAGE-190.0
ESSEX, MASS.
© WALTER E. CHANNING 1972

Whale Song™

We need another
and a wiser and
perhaps a more mystical
concept of animals. Remote
from universal nature, and living by
complicated artifice, man in civilization
surveys the creature through the glass of his
knowledge and sees thereby a feather magnified
and the whole image in distortion. We patronize
them for their incompleteness, for their tragic fate
of having taken form so far below ourselves. And
therein we err, and greatly err. For the animal shall
not be measured by man. In a world older and more
complete than ours, they move finished and complete, gifted with extensions of the senses we
have lost or never attained, living by voices we
shall never hear. They are not brethren, they
are not underlings; they are other nations,
caught with ourselves in the net of life
and time, fellow prisoners of the
splendor and travail of the earth.

Henry Beston, *The Outermost House*

Carved wooden figurehead from a New Bedford vessel circa early to mid-1800s. On display at Honolulu's Hawai'i Maritime Center.

Whale Song

The Story of Hawai'i and the Whales

Researched, Written, and Co-designed by
  MacKinnon Simpson

Edited, Art Directed, and Photographed by
  Robert B. Goodman

Managing Editor
  Lorie Rapkin

Calligraphy by
  Robert Slimbach

Typeface Design by
  Sumner Stone

Printed under the direction of
  Char and Byron Liske

Beyond Words Publishing Company Honolulu, Hawaii

PUBLISHER
BEYOND WORDS PUBLISHING COMPANY
112 Meleana Place
Honolulu, Hawaii 96817   (808) 595-3118
Toll Free 1-800-WHALE 89 • FAX 808-595-4252

Graphic production, in association with
Belknap Productions of Honolulu, and
special consultants Ken Kimura and Joel Lovingfoss.

Library of Congress Catalog Card
Number 86-72773
First edition,   November 1986
Second edition, November 1989

Printed in the United States by
Dynagraphics, Inc.
300 NW 14th
Portland, Oregon 97209

CREDITS

    WhaleSong was the first coffee-table book created with desktop
publishing tools — entirely designed, typeset, assembled, proofed
and readied for press on Apple's **Macintosh Plus** computer. This
second edition was created with the newest desktop technology
including **Macintosh II** computers, **SiClone** accelerator boards,
Radius color and gray-scale monitors with their **PrecisionColor
Calibrator** and **QuickColor** RISC based screen accelerators, **Colby
Systems'** incomparable **WalkMac**, and the **SyQuest** removable 45
megabyte drives and **Infinity** magneto-optical removable cartridge
drives from **PLI.**

    Sharp's JX-450 flatbed 300 dpi and the new **Sharp 600** dpi
color scanner was used for flat art and large transparencies. Thirty-
five millimeter film was scanned on the **Barneyscan V3.** Black and
white pictures were scanned on the **Hewlett Packard ScanJet Plus**
and **Apple** scanner. Final proofing was on the **QMS 810 and QMS
ColorScript 100.** All color calls were in **Pantone's new electronic
PMS** color system.

    A host of peripherals to make computing easier and safer came
from **Kensington.** The color software was an Alpha version of
Adobe's new **Photoshop** color retouching program and its **color
separation routines.** Other graphic software used was **Adobe's
Illustrator 88 & Streamline,** as well as Broderbund's **TypeStyler**
and **Aldus FreeHand.**

    Aldus PageMaker 3.02 with **Color Extension** was used for page
layout. **TextPert 3.01** and the **ScanJet Plus** were used to OCR the
original pages. *WhaleSong* is set in **Adobe's Stone Serif** with title
page and chapter titles calligraphed by **Robert Slimbach. Adobe
Type Manager** was used throughout the project for precise type
placement and design. Final output was to the new **RIP 3 Linotronic
L-300.** Proofing for our printer was done with **3M Color Key** and
Matchprint, as well as **nuARC** and **Burgess** technology. Color reproductions not created on the desktop were scanned with Crosfield
equipment by **Litho Color** in Honolulu, Hawaii. **Farallon's Portable
Pack PhoneNET Connectors** and **Timbuktu/Remote,** as well as
their **StarController and "Eithernet"** proved indispensable. **Weyerhaeuser's** new electro-imaging paper, **First Choice,** was used
routinely for all promotional correspondence.

Table of Contents

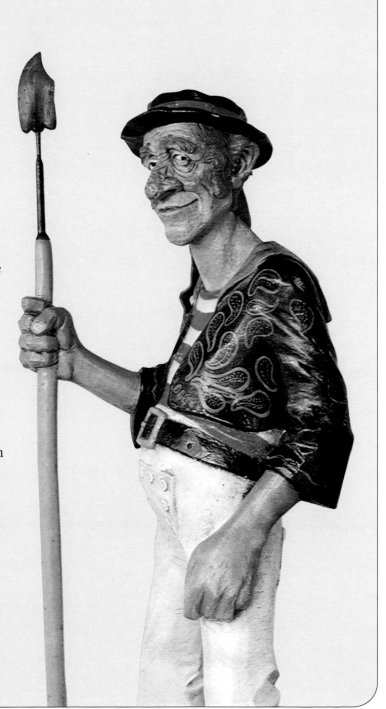

Preface

10 The Whale

14 The Early Days

18 Yankee Whalemen
    All in a Day's Work

30 'Round the Horn
    Stormy Passage

36 The Hawaiian Islands
    Panorama
    A Family Touch

50 Scrimshaw
    Sandwich Islands Banjo
    The Master and his tools
    Day by Day by Day

78 Whaling Crews
    The Whaleboat
    Greener's Gun
    Hunter, Factory, Warehouse, Home
    The *Kutusoff*

96 Hawai'i Calls
    The Kanaka Connection
    A Whaling Family
    The First Whaleship Photo
    An Historic Rescue Mission

110 Danger in the Arctic

116 Hunters Become the Hunted
    Save the Whales
    International Whaling Commission
    Pirate Whalers
    Stripmining the Sea

126 Dolphin Mind

130 The Whale's Song

142 About This Book

144 The Lahaina Whaling Museum

145 Glossary

147 Index

This second edition of WhaleSong is dedicated to my wife Debbie and children Malia and Alika, for their unflagging love, support, and understanding; to my cousin Hazel Brill Jackson, an encouraging and creative influence all my life; to my in-laws, Margaret and Ralph Dobbins, who are still putting up with me after nineteen years; and to Rick Ralston, whose generosity and sense of history made this all possible.

Preface

The Hawaiian Islands are the most remote islands on Earth. This very remoteness made them the last major landform to be discovered by 18th century European navigators — and situated them perfectly to provision the Yankee whaleships which would search the reaches of the Pacific for the Leviathan.

The year was 1819, and it would prove to be a momentous one. Kamehameha the Great had died, and both the Hawaiian religion and its ancient social order died with him. Missionaries with a new religion and a new social order were on their way, intent on imposing their gloomy Calvinist tenets on a happy people. The first rowdy Yankee whalers put in at Lahaina, where they heard news of thousands of sperm whales for the taking in the Sea of Japan.

Whaling was to change these Islands forever. The licentious whalers, carousing through Lahaina and Honolulu in search of girls and grog, demonstrated their conviction that there was "no God west of the Horn." Just as fervently, the missionaries believed that they had *brought* God round the Horn on the brig *Thaddeus*, and that He was now in residence. Even that did not deter the whalers as they battled with the missionaries — at least once with cannon.

Economically, Hawai'i's growth for over fifty years would depend on the servicing of whaleships, and many of the Islands' most influential businesses of today began as purveyors to the whaling industry. But half a century was all that it would last, by the 1860s, the War Between the States, the discovery of petroleum in Pennsylvania, and the scarcity of whales doomed the whaling business. The final blow came in 1871 when the last remnants of the Pacific Fleet were crushed in an early Arctic freeze, an act of God from which the industry would never recover.

The Hawaiian Islands, whose fragile economy had depended upon sandalwood and then whaling, was rescued — just in time — by sugar. Honolulu, with its natural harbor, grew and prospered into a major commercial center. Lahaina, on the other hand, became a backwater and languished in Maui's warm sun almost a century before being invaded again, recently by 'whalers' who use telephotos instead of harpoons. From the brink of extinction, the whales too are back, and enjoy man's newfound interest in protecting them.

This book, commissioned by the Lahaina Whaling Museum, brings together old paintings and lithographs, letters, and daguerrotypes, documents and stories, many never before published. To these treasures are added contemporary images depicting the beauty of the whale and the story of marine mammal conservation.

8

Mai ka pō mai, hānau ke kaiuli,

Mai ka pō mai, hānau ke akua,

Ua hānai ʻia e ka moana

Ma ka hohonu ā ke ākea

I kona ʻano maoli hoʻokino iho ke akua,

I loko o ke kai loloa kona ola,

ʻO Kanaloa,

ʻO ka palaoa.

Out of night, born the sea.
Out of night, born the God.
Nurtured by the oceans,
Deep and vast his domain.
Into his true nature he formed himself...
Life enduring in the sea.
O, Kanaloa
O, ivory-toothed whale.

Adapted by Kawena Johnson from the *Kumulipo*, a Hawaiian creation chant.

The Whale

Life itself bubbled from the cauldron of our ancient seas. Simple lifeforms became ever more complex. Dinosaurs evolved, then dissolved into fossils and footprints. Continents and oceans exchanged places as glaciers crept from their polar homes, scouring lakes and depositing mountains. Reptiles, amphibians, mammals and birds shared the earth with an ever-changing cast of plants and insects.

*P*erhaps sixty million years ago, a four-legged land mammal returned to the sea, from whence its ancestors had wriggled timeless eons before. Over millions of evolutionary years, its front legs streamlined into pectoral fins, the hind legs shrank from disuse and then vanished altogether, the ropelike tail transformed into powerful horizontal flukes and its thick coat of insulating hair became a layer of blubber. Weightless in the salted water, the creatures grew, heavier than a dozen bull elephants, larger by far than even the thundering Brontosaurus of the Mesozoic Era. The great whales today are the largest creatures ever to exist on earth.

Two primary sub-orders of whales swim in today's oceans, the Mysticeti ("mustached whales") and the Odontoceti ("toothed whales"). The Mysticeti, like humpbacks, blues and right whales, have supple stalks of fringed baleen as filters in their enormous mouths and two nostrils (or blowholes). The Odontoceti have teeth instead of baleen, and one blowhole instead of two. This group includes sperm whales, dolphins and porpoises. Within the two groups, there are immense differences in size, social order, diet and geographic distribution. Whales range throughout the Pacific Ocean from the icy seas near the Poles to the temperate waters near the Equator.

Left: *Deep off the Kona Coast of Hawai'i, a singing male humpback, hangs motionless, unaware of the photographer.*

Whales of the Pacific

Blue (1): rorqual; baleen; closely related to the Fin whale; largest living thing ever to exist on earth, bigger than 30 elephants, far larger than even the Brotosaurus; hunted only in the 20th century; the future for blue whales is questionable as there may not be enough breeding stock left.

Sperm (2): toothed; hunted extensively in both the 19th and 20th centuries for fine oil, spermaceti and ambergris; can dive to a depth of at least two miles and hold its breath for over an hour; ivory teeth used for scrimshaw; has the largest, most complex brain in the world; may hunt using sonic booms to stun its prey, which are primarily giant squid; the population numbers are relatively safe.

Right (3): baleen; named by whalers because it was the 'right' whale to hunt; the population has been almost exterminated and the future is uncertain; an Arctic cousin, the Bowhead, has baleen up to 14' long and is still legally hunted by the Eskimos.

Humpback (4): baleen; most-studied great whale; one Pacific population migrates annually from Alaskan feeding grounds to warm Hawaiian waters for mating and calving; famous for both acrobatic leaps and extremely complex songs.

Narwhal (5): toothed; twisted 'unicorn horn' on male is really a tooth which is extremely valuable; lives in cold waters around the North Pole.

Pilot (6): toothed; supposedly named because it guided mariners to safe anchorages; occasionally demonstrates still-unexplained mass beachings.

Orca (9): toothed; common name Killer Whale; will attack, kill and eat great whales and polar bears, however it is gentle with human beings.

Beluga (7): toothed; its name means "white one" in Russian because of its unique cream-white skin color.

Gray (8): baleen; often hunted from shore stations along the West Coast; called Devil Fish by whalers because of ferocity, these are actually quite gentle whales (unless harpooned); their numbers have been rising.

The Early Days

For ages man had watched the giant whales spout at sea, and scavenged those which washed ashore. But the first men to grab their bone-tipped spears and launch canoes in pursuit of the great beast must have been both very brave and very hungry. In canoes with outriggers, canoes hollowed from logs, canoes stitched of birchbark or walrus-hide, men from the Equator to the Poles set out to slay the Great Whales.

*L*ike man, whales are warm-blooded, suckle their young, and draw breath from the atmosphere. This last kinship with man made whales vulnerable, for their vapor spout and their incredible bulk made them easy to see from land. At first it was just chance that someone on the beach spotted a whale out to sea, but later, men would erect cleated poles and station look-outs to scan the horizon for the telltale spout.

The methods of these early whale hunters were simple and direct: drive the whale to the shallows and kill him there, or harpoon the creature with barbed spear attached to a wooden float. As the whale dragged this 'drogue' around, the leviathan would grow exhausted (as would, presumably, the whalemen rowing furiously in pursuit).

When the whale slowed, it would be killed with a lance, and then, as if chasing and killing the behemoth weren't strenuous enough, the whalers hitched a rope to the tail of their immense prey and towed it to the land station for processing. The blubber was peeled off ('flensed'), then boiled down ('tryed out') in huge cast iron pots to make oil for their lamps.

Left: A humpback breaches off Ka'anapali, Maui in this contemporary painting by Herb Kawainui Kane. A Hawaiian double-hull canoe sails alongside the whaleship Sunbeam *out of New Bedford.*

15

The most sophisticated early whalers, Basques from the coasts of Spain and France, sailed as far as Canada in the 1500s, and perhaps earlier, to set up summer whaling stations. Casks brimming with oil, they would return each fall to Europe's lucrative markets.

Indians from both northern coasts of America, as well as Eskimos, Europeans, Asians, and South Sea islanders all hunted whales from shore. The most accomplished ocean people of all, early Hawaiians, did not hunt whales, probably because their religion recognized the whale as a representation of Kanaloa, God of the Sea. The Hawaiians' sophisticated agriculture and aquaculture made the whale unnecessary as food, and their lamp oil came from the sacred kukui nut. While the Hawaiians did strip beached whales — one badge of rank, the *lei niho palaoa,* was made from a sperm whale's ivory tooth — they did not put out from shore to hunt the whale.

Land whaling was, however, practiced by New England's original settlers, the Indians of the Algonquin nation. And the droves of early white Colonists — following the original pilgrims from Europe — were certainly aware of the practice as well. The Royal Charter issued by King James I to the Plymouth "Mayflower" Colony in 1620 granted these settlers "all royal fishes, whales, balan, sturgeons and other fishes." These sturdy Yankees would waste little time in establishing the greatest whaling industry the world had ever seen.

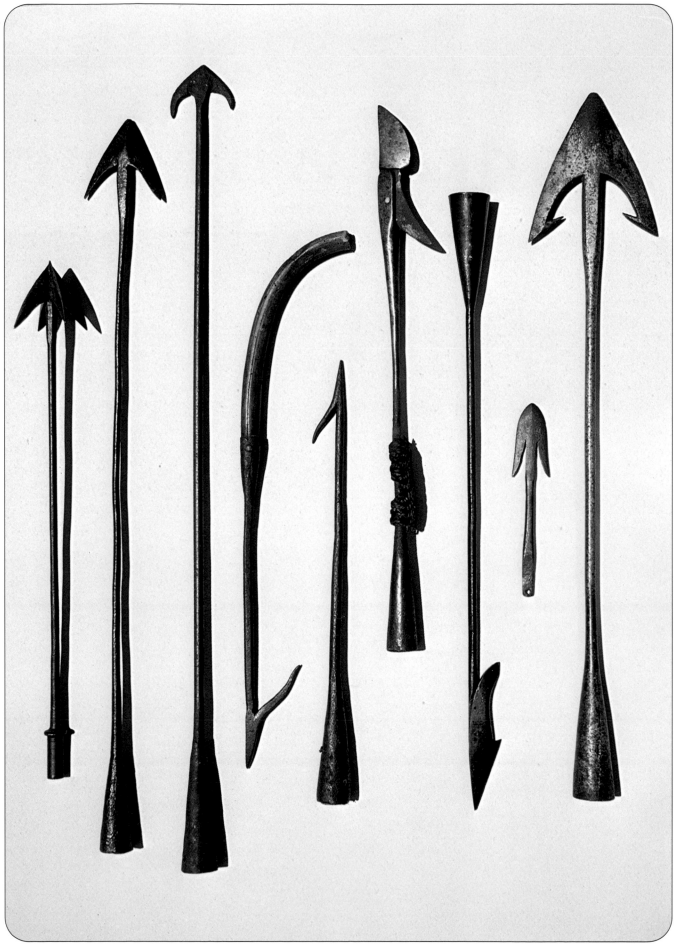

Yankee Whalemen

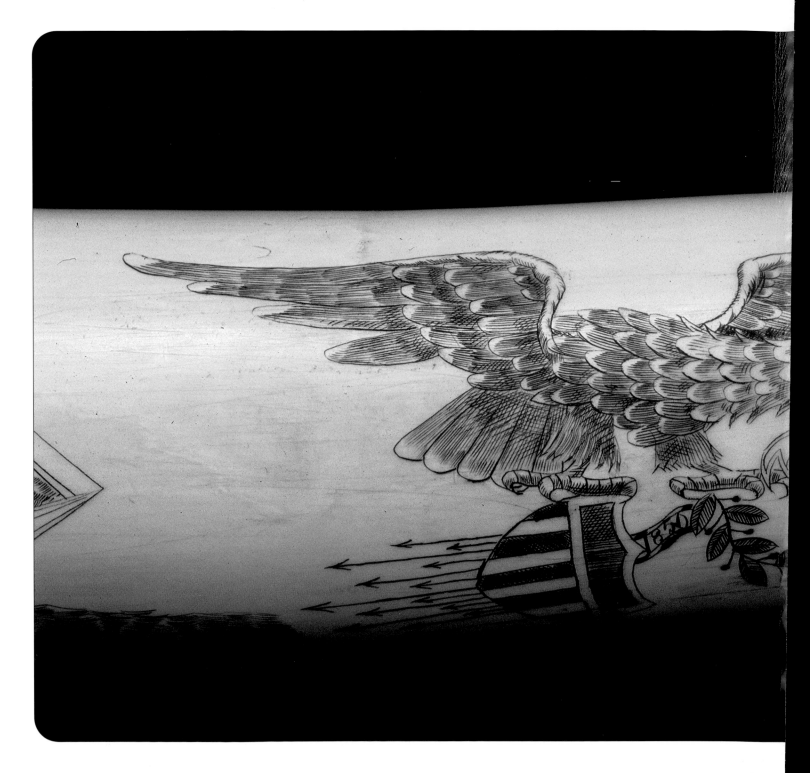

Their very existence bespoke a great and grand adventure. They had yanked up roots in the old country and were boldly conquering a new wilderness. Nothing — not hostile Indians, not the King of England, not impenetrable forest nor uncharted seas — would stand in their way.

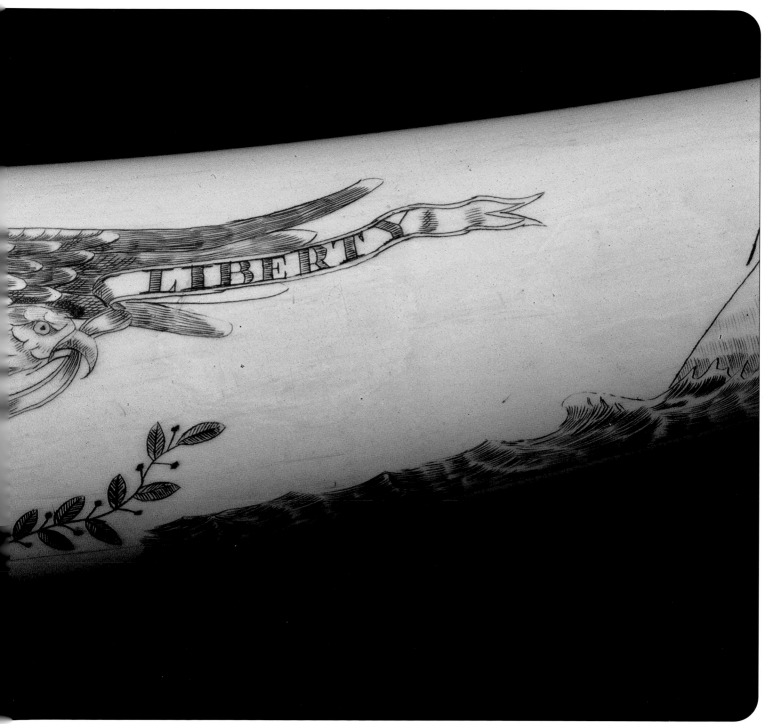

Scrimshawed tusk from the Lahaina Whaling Museum

While the Mayflower pilgrim charter granted them "all royal fishes," the first white men to actually go whaling in the New World were from the north shore of Long Island, around 1650. Land whaling quickly spread the few miles across Long Island Sound to the tiny seaports of Connecticut and Massachusetts. Nantucket — the name means "a far away place" in the Wampanoag tongue — is a lonely, sandy island some twenty miles off Cape Cod. Peopled mostly by Quakers escaping Puritan persecution on the mainland, Nantucket came somewhat late to the game of hunting whales. In fact, the first whale caught there was taken only because it stayed in the harbor for some three days — time enough for a local blacksmith to fashion a harpoon in his forge.

In his tome of 1760, *The History of Nantucket*, Obed Macy related, "In the year 1690 some persons were on a high hill observing the whales spouting and sporting with each other, when one observed; there — pointing to the sea — is a green pasture where our children's grandchildren will go for bread."

A correct prognostication if ever there was one, for Nantucket would quickly become the center of the colonies' whaling industry. Before 1700, the Nantucket fishermen hired one Ichabod Paddock, a land whaler from Cape Cod, to cross the Channel and teach them to hunt whales. Paddock set up four whaling stations with lookout towers spaced across the south shore of the Island, and trained six-man crews to run each one.

Soon Nantucket became an extremely successful whaling community, and her whalers began to leave their towers and range out into the ocean in small sloops. At this time — the early 1700s — the whalers pursued the right whale (so named because it was the 'right whale' to catch). It was slow, floated when dead, and provided a great deal of oil — three tremendous advantages to these early whalers.

Around 1700, a sperm whale had washed up on a Nantucket beach. It was about the same size as the right whale, but its oil was much finer, a large cavity in the nose was filled with the waxlike spermaceti which made excellent candles, and the lower jaw was lined with large ivory teeth. It was a better catch than the right whale, but Nantucketers had never seen one like it before, so they assumed it had strayed there from unknown environs.

Right: The crew of the whaleship Margaret *out of New London poses on deck for the camera in this rare photograph. Captain J.W. Buddington is seated front and center.*

Mystic Seaport Museum

21

Then one day in 1712, so the story goes, Captain Christopher Hussey was sailing his small sloop in search of right whales when a sudden squall blew up and drove him far out to sea — smack into a herd of sperm whales. Storm or no storm, Hussey sensed an opportunity for profit, so he selected the largest one and harpooned the great creature. His sloop rode out the storm in the lee of their huge victim, and once the storm abated, Hussey towed his prize to Nantucket for processing in the tryworks on shore.

Captain Hussey had accidentally discovered that the sperm whale lived well out in the open ocean — a discovery that would change the whaling industry forever. Slowly but surely, offshore whaling would replace land whaling, and that development would later impact a small chain of isolated volcanic islands a quarter of the globe away.

Chasing the sperm whales further and further offshore necessitated some major changes in both the vessels and methodology. Suddenly, it made little sense to pursue a whale all the way to Newfoundland if, after killing it, one had to laboriously tow the hulk all the way back to Nantucket for trying out. So the whalers would peel off the blubber, pack it tightly in casks, and continue hunting until the holds were full.

The next step — the addition of tryworks right on deck — came quickly, so the processing of blubber into oil and then barreling it could be done on the spot. This combination of the heavy try-pots and the resulting storage of casks of oil, as well as the longer voyages in rougher seas offshore, required sturdier ships than the light sloops which Hussey and his peers had used. Thus were born the first whaleships, almost universally acclaimed the ugliest craft ever to float. They were stubby and stout and prodigiously slow, but perfectly suited to the task at hand.

Left: Right whales are filter-feeders, with long flexible plates of fringed baleen ('whalebone') affixed to the upper jaw. They feed near the surface on small marine organisms called "krill." Right whales' most distinguishing features are the patches of thick callus on the head — home to parasites and barnacles. The species is wide-ranging, but has been so ravaged by hunting that sightings are now rare. This painting of a right whale cow and her calf is by Richard Ellis.

RICHARD ELLIS

24

Somewhere, roaming the oceans of Earth, may well be an old bull sperm whale with a scar long-healed from the bite of a New England whaleman's harpoon. The last whaleship docked in New Bedford in 1922, so it is not a stretch of the imagination that a whale chased then still swims free.

The spermaceti, a toothed whale, bears the largest and most convoluted brain ever to exist on Planet Earth, bar none. He feeds at great depths, has been tracked on sonar diving to a depth of two miles, and may well have the capacity to stun or kill a prospective meal by triggering an underwater sonic boom using the reservoir of liquid wax, together with the complex system of valves and tubes in his proboscis. To the whalers, the sperms were a far more dangerous foe than the somewhat lethargic right whale. The sperm's blubber oil was so fine that the whalers kept it in marked casks, for it traditionally brought two to three times the price of oil from other whales. Spermaceti wax was finer still, for candles and as a lubricant. And there was always the chance to find ambergris — a compacted clump of matter found in the large intestine, prized as a fixative in perfume and worth up to $15 an ounce — a fortune in the 1800s. The fifty or so ivory teeth, which whalers scrimshawed, had no other value.

In his masterpiece, *Moby Dick*, Herman Melville wrote, "The sperm whale, scientific or poetic, lives not complete in any literature. Far above all other hunted whales, his is an unwritten life." That is as true today as when Melville penned it in 1851. In the ensuing 135 plus years, man has invented television, split the atom, strolled on the moon, and still the sperm whale's "is an unwritten life."

We best know him as a creature of legend: the lone renegade bull prowling the oceans in search of whaleships to ram; as the Great Leviathan swallowing Jonah and Pinocchio (though not simultaneously); as the immense challenger of the ferocious ten-armed Giant Squid. The sperm is the whale which comes to mind when we think of 'whale.' And he is also the whale we know all too well in death — how many barrels of spermaceti and oil he yielded — but know hardly at all in life.

Above: The Harpooneer. Adapted from an original linoleum print by Lowell LeRoy Balcom, 1839.
Left: A herd of juvenile and adult sperm whales. At 60 feet in length and up to 120,000 pounds in weight, the bull was twice the size of the cow. Painting by Richard Ellis.

Above: Tryworks bailer. Adapted from a linoleum print by Lowell LeRoy Balcom, 1839.

A whaleship performed well three disparate functions: she was hunter, factory and warehouse all in one. She sailed the Seven Seas in search of whales, from Pole to Pole and everywhere in between.

Assembled from huge timbers culled from New England's primeval forests, Yankee whaleships were the best in the world. Bulky by design and broad of beam, the whaleships were ponderous in the water. The cedar whaleboats she carried to pursue the prey were, on the other hand, sleek and maneuverable.

Right whales were captured by harpooning them with a line roped to a wooden float — often an empty sealed barrel — which they would drag around until exhausted. Sperm whales were more active, so the whaleboat itself became the float, and when the harpoon stuck fast, the carefully coiled line whipped out — oftentimes more than a half-mile of it — from its oaken tub. The ensuing tow was nicknamed the Nantucket Sleigh Ride.

The Americans — who at this time, of course, still thought of themselves as Colonists — demonstrated their Yankee Ingenuity by starting whaling late but almost immediately improving upon its techniques and equipment. By the early 1750s, the upstart New Englanders were not only filling the colonies' needs for whale oil, they were exporting their surplus to Great Britain — and actually providing more than the Mother Country's own fleet.

By 1755, the abilities of these persistant New England whalers had so impressed Edmund Burke — to this day still considered the finest orator to ever serve in Parliament — that in his most famous speech he said, "Look at the manner in which the people of New England have of late carried on the whale fishery. We follow them amongst the tumbling mountains of ice...Nor is the equinoctal heat more discouraging to them, than the accumulated winter of both poles. Whilst some of them draw the line and strike the harpoon on the coast of Africa, others run the longitude, and pursue their giant game along the coast of Brazil. No sea but what is vexed by their fisheries. No climate that is not witness to their toils. Neither the perseverance of Holland, nor the activity of France, nor the dexterous and firm sagacity of English enterprise, ever carried this most perilous mode of hardy industry to the extent to which it has been pushed by this recent people..."

At the time of Burke's 1755 Parliament speech, whaling had spread to seaports up and down the New England coast and was just being established in the small Massachusetts town of New Bedford, which was destined to eventually replace Nantucket as the colonies' whaling center. A persistent sandbar across the mouth of Nantucket Harbor would deny passage there to the larger whaleships.

By 1774 — a year before the American Revolution began — the colonies had 360 whaleships, 300 of which were from Massachusetts (and half of those from Nantucket). The fortunes of the industry were expanding, as were the distances the whalers were travelling. American whaleships regularly hunted in the South Atlantic, occasionally venturing south as far as the Falkland Islands off the coast of Argentina, some 8000 miles from home and barely a thousand from Antarctica. And *this* in 1774!

The American Revolution wrought havoc on the New England whalemen. Their fleets were almost annihilated by the British Navy, which set out to sink everything that floated. New Bedford, which began the war with almost fifty whaleships, lost thirty-four of them in a single raid plotted by Sir Henry Clinton.

Below: A very early lithograph, dated 1813, and titled "A Ship's Boat Attacking A Whale." Most whalers did wear hats though they were otherwise not quite so nattily dressed.

Nantucketers were especially hard hit. In an effort to continue whaling, they declared the island neutral, and were thus prey both to the British and to angry Patriots as well. By 1783, when hostilities ceased, Nantucket had lost 149 of her 150 whaleships, and more than one-fourth of the 800 families on the island had a widow as head of household.

The British whaling fleet, of course, expanded during the war, and when the Americans began to revive their trade with Britain, they were hit with a stiff duty of 18£ per ton, a tax which made their efforts unprofitable. For a time, American whalers simply eked out an existence as their business slowly improved. By the late 1780s, both the British and American fleets ruled the southern Atlantic.

In January 1789, the British whaleship *Emilia* rounded Cape Horn and became the first whaler to enter the South Pacific. It was a trip, 'round the Horn,' that would be repeated many thousands of times in the next century. And thirty years hence, the first whaleships would land at the Sandwich Islands and change the course of Hawaiian history forever.

Lahaina Whaling Museum

*"The Spermacetti Whale found by the
Nantucketois, is an active and fierce animal,
and requires vast address and boldness in
the fisherman."*

Thomas Jefferson, 1778

All in a Day's Work

Active and fierce animal indeed! Each time the lofty lookout cried, "She blows," each time a whaleboat was lowered into the sea in pursuit of a whale, each time the harpoon's iron fang sank into blubber, men risked their very lives. Hunting the sperm whale — or any whale — was a task for the inordinately brave, or foolhardy, or dense. Imagine for a moment being in the third seat of a sleek, double-ended whaleboat, skinned with cedar planking less than a half inch thick. You are pulling hard on an 18' oar, in unison with five other men, as the mate hollers cadence, orders and expletives.

You are headed, backwards, towards an "active and fierce animal" who may outweigh you *and* your boatload of linetubs, harpoons and sailors by some 119,000 pounds. A creature in *his* element, who can fill his lungs with air and dive more than two miles straight down. And a creature who can crush your flimsy craft with one sweep of his tailflukes or one snap of his ivory-studded jaws.

As your boat nears its immense prey — a quarry that you still have not seen as your seat faces the direction from whence you came — the crusty harpooneer lays down his oar and clambers to the prow. Do you *really* want him to launch his iron spear? Do you *really* think that your measly share of the voyage profits (your "lay") is worth what may well happen next? Forget the ungodly conditions in the fo'c's'le, the wormy food, the back-breaking work trying out the oil, the hours of boredom, the loneliness. Forget all that. Remember the harpooneer crouched in the bow of this slender rocking boat, waiting for just the right moment to pierce the Leviathan's flank.

Remember the fear — the terror even — waiting to know whether this whale will be the one to turn and fight, to focus his anger and surprise to crush you lifeless in the roiling sea. What could be worth that? Whale oil? Spermaceti? Ambergris? Ivory teeth for scrimshaw? Adventure?

The log of the whaleship *Brewster* says it best: "My opinion is that any man who has a log hut on land with a corn cake at the fire and would consent to leave them to come...on a whale voyage is a proper subject for a lunatic asylum."

Left: "All in a Day's Work" is an 1877 oil study by Charles S. Raleigh for a much larger panorama. From the collection of the Kendall Whaling Museum.

Everyone connected with each whaling voyage was at risk. Ship owners gambled many thousands of dollars to outfit a vessel and then had to wait some four years in hopes that it would return with its holds full. A few ships, like the *Charles W. Morgan*, came back again and again (in the *Morgan's* case, thirty-seven times over eighty years!), while others left New Bedford or Nantucket on their maiden voyage and vanished over the horizon without a trace. Great as an owners' risk was, of course, the men aboard were gambling with their very lives. Just what were the prizes they were gambling for?

Whales yielded four marketable products: whale oil from the blubber; 'whalebone' from the baleen whales; and spermaceti and occasionally ambergris from the sperm whale. The profits from the sale of these raw materials were divided between the ship owner (who generally got about 66%) and the whaling crew and officers — each of whom got a percentage, or "lay." The master was the highest paid with a lay of perhaps 1/17 (about 6%), the three mates were next, then the skilled harpooneers and finally, with a lay as low as 1/220 (less than half of one percent) were the forecastle hands. On a voyage lasting four years and netting $100,000, for example, the owner would get $66,000, the master about $6000, the mates perhaps $4000, the harpooneers some $2000 and a crewman about $400! So for investing four hard years of risking your life chasing whales across the open ocean, you have pocketed some twenty-seven cents a day!

It is little wonder that it became increasingly difficult to assemble competent crews and that the percentage of psychotics, fugitives and the befuddled occupying the fo'c's'le kept increasing. As other, better, opportunities presented themselves — factory jobs in New England, free land out west, and gold, to name just three — fewer and fewer men signed up and more were 'recruited.' And more and more of these jumped ship whenever a landfall was sighted. They were replaced by earlier deserters from other whaleships, who had grown tired of beachcombing, and — especially in Hawai'i's case — by local lads.

But no matter who rowed the whaleboats and harpooned the whales and cut up the blubber and tried out the oil, whaling was a godawful dangerous job with extremely high risk, extremely low wages, and years and years away from home.

'Round the Horn

Lahaina Whaling Museum

Take one part waves rushing westward across thousands of miles of open Pacific. Add one part waves rushing eastward across thousands of miles of open Atlantic. Mix both together in a narrow, constricting channel. Garnish with biting cold wind, floating icebergs, a coastline shrouded in fog, and storms swirling off the nether reaches of the South Pole. Serve to an exhausted, frightened crew aboard a pitching, tossing whaleship.

*T*he voyage of *Emilia,* the first whaleship to 'round the Horn' into the Pacific, signaled a new era in the hunt for the whale. The Pacific Ocean covers some one-third of the Earth's surface, and just getting there around Cape Horn was an 8000 mile voyage of several month's duration from New England. Going the *other* way, around Africa's Cape of Good Hope, took even longer. And the canal across the Isthmus of Panama would not be dug until 1914. So the only practical route into the Pacific for the whaleships of the 19th century was the same one *Emilia* took in 1789 — around Cape Horn, the southernmost tip of the South American continent.

The passage 'round the Horn' was always treated with both awe and dread by the sailors who had to undertake it. The trip was almost always rough and stormy, as the currents from the two oceans churned headlong into each other in the narrow passage between the Cape and Antarctica. Frigid winds whirled constantly from the South Pole, making the voyage under sail even more dangerous and uncomfortable. One captain's wife wrote in her journal, "We made 20 knots today — 10 straight ahead and 10 up and down." The trip was choppy even in a long, sleek ship like a Clipper — in a short, tubby whaleship, it was awful. But it was a journey which had to be made to follow the whales, just as some seventy years later, whalers would brave the hostile Arctic Ocean in pursuit of their prey.

Stormy Passage

From the collection of Robert Van Dyke

One memorable account of a storm-tossed whaleship voyage comes down to us not from a whaler's log, but from a young missionary aboard the whaleship *Thames*. The year was 1823 and the *Thames* had left New Haven two months before carrying the Second Company of missionaries bound for the Sandwich Islands. As the whaleship hugged the coastline of Argentina on her way to Cape Horn, she was struck by a hurricane off Rio del Plata. Reverend Charles S. Stewart's words follow:

Jan 25, S. lat. 37°, W. long. 52° 48'. It came raging so suddenly upon us, that the Captain had time only to exclaim — "All hands on deck! Hand the royals and the top-gallent sails too! Clew up the mainsail! Mind your helm, Quick! Quick!" — while all became vociferation and confusion — before the wind struck us a full broadside, and instantly laid the ship almost on her beam ends. Everything cracked in her struggle against the blast, and she shot forward like a race-horse, with her gunnels in the water, and the waves on her lee towering yard-arm high. The howling of the tempest — plunging of the vessel! —and trampling and hallooing of the sailors effectually prevented our taking any rest. The first person from the deck reported the wind to be a hurricane and the waves mountain high: which we were ready to believe without ocular demonstration. One or two, only of the passengers attempted to take breakfast. While at the table, a sea struck the ship along her whole length, from the quarterdeck to the bows; &

the water came pouring down the hogs-head, down the companion-way, and through the steerage hatch. Everything was swept from the table, and some of the family, mattresses and all, were thrown from their berths into the cabin, and those below, thinking the vessel going down, rushed on deck with looks and exclamations of horror. On deck, one of the boats was stove, and the ship, in its whole length, was washed by the wave.

The gale continued to increase, and the sea to rise at a fearful rate, it became necessary, for our safety, to have the upper yards and masts sent down. The seamen were obliged to mount to their very tops, to unloose the rigging; where, they were swung, with incredible velocity through a space of little less than ninety feet; while an inevitable grave yawned beneath them, should the slender yard to which they clung give way or they themselves once lose their footing. The unnatural sound of their voices, as their screams to make themselves heard below were caught by the wind and borne away on the tempest, came to the ear like the shrieks of the dying; and I dared scarce look up for a moment lest I see someone thrown into the raging sea, where no power of man could have brought him rescue.

The storm raged till evening with unabated violence. Whatever the degree of danger may have been, the scene was of a character, deeply, to fix thoughts of that event by which, sooner or later, we shall all be made to stand before the bar of God.

Emilia returned to London in 1790 with close to 150 tons of sperm oil in her holds and tales of great hunting off Peru. The British promptly dispatched more whaleships to the new Pacific Grounds, and the Americans soon followed. Two years later, in 1791, *Beaver, Washington, Hector* , and *Rebecca* — all from Nantucket — were the first Yankee whalers around the Horn. Soon, American whaling interests so dominated the South Pacific that it became known as American Polynesia, but this domination would be sternly challenged by another war.

Wars always proved to be serious setbacks for the whale-hunters — their ponderous ships were inviting prey for the heavily-armed men-of-war prowling the seas. The War of 1812 was no exception.

Little remembered today, the War of 1812 was a confrontation between Great Britain and the United States of such monumental stupidity that historians are still — more than 170 years later — arguing over how it came about. Certainly slow communication was one factor: the British agreed, in London, to the repeal of the laws which were the root cause of the conflict — two days before war was declared in Washington! This war may well have been the only one in which both sides still insist they were victorious, or in which the most important battle was fought fifteen days after the peace treaty was signed!

Perhaps the only memorable thing to come out of the entire sordid affair was "The Star-Spangled Banner," penned by Francis Scott Key, to the tune, ironically, of an old English drinking song.

For the whalers, the War of 1812 was a complete disaster, just as the Revolution had been thirty years earlier and the Civil War would be fifty years hence. Whaleships were slow and for the most part carried only harpoons, never much of a match for cannonballs. Whaling vessels were sunk, captured on the high seas or just blockaded in their ports. Nantucketers again opposed the war, and for good reason: they began it with 120 whaleships and ended it, two years later, with twenty-three. Even British whalers took their lumps — the U.S. frigate *Essex* rounded the Horn and captured a dozen astonished whaleships flying the Union Jack — a blow from which the British whaling industry never recovered.

When peace was finally declared, on Christmas Eve 1814, the whalers could get back to business. This time recovery was swift, and the Pacific once again teemed with whale hunters, who were still 'working' below the Equator in search of their prey. After originally hunting along the coasts of Chile and Peru, they ventured west to Australia, New Zealand and the islands of Oceania. Hawai'i still lay far to the north of the whaling fleets.

Lahaina Whaling Museum

The first Western ship known to have touched the Hawaiian Islands was the *Resolution* under Captain Cook in 1778 and 1779. The first trading ship to arrive was laden with furs and headed for China, in 1785. No whaleship would visit these shores until September 1819, when two Yankee vessels — *Balena* and *Equator* — would appear together. This was fully thirty years after *Emilia* first ventured into Pacific waters. The time lag was due primarily to Hawai'i's location: at 20 degrees North of the Equator, the Islands were fully one quarter of the globe from Drake's Passage around Cape Horn. That is a tremendous amount of ocean, especially since the ships were filling their holds with whale oil in the South Pacific. It literally took the whalers that thirty years to kill or frighten away enough whales in the south that they *needed* to hunt in the North Pacific.

A report came from a sandalwood trader that he had seen huge herds of sperm whales off Japan, and the number of whaleships approaching the Hawaiian Islands increased dramatically. Distances from New England (and Olde England) had become so great that the process of whaling had to change once again.

From the original day voyages of small sloops whaling off Nantucket in the early 1700s, to the half-year voyages to the South Atlantic in the 1770s, to the full-year voyages into the South Pacific in the early 1800s, the whalers had continuously increased their range. Just getting to Hawai'i took almost a year, at five months each way. Whaleships increased in size to make their journeys more profitable and, at the same time, increased their time 'on station' and hence the length of their voyage.

By the mid-1800s, whalers were often gone from their homeport for as long as five years. Despite the sailor's superstition of not allowing women on board, many captains brought their wives and their young children along. Often these families would take up residence in Hawai'i, while their husbands were off chasing Leviathans to the North.

Lahaina Whaling Museum

The Hawaiian Islands

New Bedford Whaling Museum

"Midway across the North Pacific, space, time, and life uniquely interlace a chain of islands... These small fragments of land appear offered to sky by water and pressed to Earth by stars."

Charles A. Lindbergh

*T*he chain of Hawaiian islands — all 132 of them — evolved in a 1600 mile-long semicircle over the past twenty-five million years. The lava that formed them belched from a volcanic hot spot in the sea floor almost four miles down, a process which continues still. Their location kept them undiscovered during the more than two centuries of Pacific exploration following Ferdinand Magellan's charter voyage. That same location made them ideal as the stopping-off place for the whaleships of the 19th century.

Whaling was excellent in the seas around Japan, but the country itself was closed to foreigners until long after the whale supply there dwindled. Next the whalers would discover great hunting in the Arctic Sea, but again, with nowhere close by to replenish their supplies. Hawai'i offered an excellent base of operations in the Pacific: to provision, to refit, and to either warehouse or transship barrels of whale oil and bales of whalebone back to market on merchant ships. Early in 1853, the clipper ship *Sovereign of the Seas* left Honolulu bound for Boston with 8000 barrels of whale oil in her cavernous holds.

Hawai'i also offered whalemen a mild climate and friendly natives, which made it a perfect place to give crews a break from the tedium of extremely long voyages on very cramped and dirty ships.

When the first two Yankee whaleships arrived in 1819, they spotted and killed a sperm whale off the Big Island. The whalers' arrival may well have been prophetic of things to come, but their catch was not. Very little whaling would actually be done in the vicinity of the Islands. There were whales here, but not in the numbers to attract a fleet of whaleships, season after season. What *did* attract them was the central location, convenient both to summer hunting in the north and winter hunting near the Equator.

Left: *Sperm whaling off Hawai'i in 1839.*

The news of sperm whales by the thousands in the Sea of Japan triggered the whalers' invasion of Hawai'i. Just three years after the first two ships arrived, in 1822, the number rose to sixty, and for the next eighteen years, Hawai'i's two major ports, Lahaina and Honolulu, would average a hundred visits a year. As the sandalwood trade faded into the dust of a terrain stripped of its fragrant trees, whaling was already there as its replacement. Quickly, the Islands became economically dependent on the whaleships to fill both public and private coffers.

The romanticized image of rum-sodden and

European explorers had repeatedly crisscrossed the Pacific on voyages of discovery for a couple of hundred years before James Cook stumbled on the Islands (and named them for his patron, the Earl of Sandwich). The Hawaiian chain, although stretching across 1600 miles of ocean and featuring several active, erupting volcanos smudging the sky red, was well away from the established trade routes and had been missed not only by the other explorers but by Spanish galleons making their annual Treasure Voyages between Mexico and the Philippines, and by China traders as well.

Lahaina Whaling Museum

lust-crazed whalers carrying off shapely native girls and/or terrorizing the good citizens of Lahaina and Honolulu certainly had some basis in truth. But the economic impact of sailors spending their meager wages "on the town" pales beside the economic impact of entire ships — by the hundreds — being provisioned for the next six months' voyage. The real dollars went to the chandlers, warehouses and shipyards servicing the whaleships, not to the grog shops and bawdyhouses servicing the whalers.

The impact of whaling on the Sandwich Islands was tremendous and literally put them "on the map."

Even after Cook's discovery, only a handful of ships a year, primarily fur traders, visited Hawai'i. In 1812, three sea-captains from Boston struck an agreement with Kamehameha the Great to export the islands' fragrant sandalwood to China, where it was coveted as incense and for carving. This trade continued until the mountain slopes and valleys were virtually denuded of the *iliahi* tree.

Even with a limited trade in sandalwood (limited not by the demand but by the supply), Hawai'i was still way off the beaten track. A few *haoles* — as the Hawaiians called foreigners — made it their home, and Hawaiians themselves travelled, usually only to replace lost crewmen on trading ships.

One such early Hawaiian traveller was a young orphan named Opukahaia who sailed to New England in 1809 aboard the *Triumph*. All alone in the seaport of New Haven, Connecticut, Opukahaia was befriended by some Yale students and soon converted to Christ — the first Hawaiian to do so. His new friends pronounced his Hawaiian name "Obookiah," and so he was baptized Henry Obookiah. A very enthusiastic convert, he helped convince the American Board of Commissioners for Foreign Missions to dis-

Henry Obookiah
Collection of Bishop Museum

patch missionaries to his homeland. Obookiah was making his own plans to join the First Company when he contracted typhus fever and died in 1818 at age 26. His death — and the immense posthumous popularity of his sanctimonious memoirs — solidified the Board in their resolve to send missionaries to the Hawaiian Islands.

Only one of the original seven selected, Daniel Chamberlain, met the Missionary Board's marriage requirement, and the other six set about in a mad scramble in search of mates willing to accompany them. The First Company's leader, Hiram Bingham, was the last to wed, just six days before sailing, to a young woman he had met but three weeks before.

Panorama

"Get your tickets now, folks. Just two bits — 25¢ — to experience three miles of thrills, a Whaling Voyage 'round the World."

*T*he scrolling panorama was a 19th century predecessor of movies. It was, quite literally, a moving picture, painted on a huge roll of canvas and then slowly hand-cranked across a theatre stage, while a narrator, accompanied by the dramatic moods of an organist, provided running commentary.

"A Whaling Voyage 'round the World" was a panorama on the grand scale created by a self-taught artist, Benjamin Russell, who spent three and a half years aboard the New Bedford whaleship *Kutusoff* making detailed drawings of her ports-of-call. Returning home in March of 1845, he enlisted one Caleb Purrington — house painter by trade — presumably to paint the ocean and sky while he did the landscapes.

It was an immense job, no matter who did what, and took the two men almost three years to complete. Next, they faced the task of filling up auditoriums, theatres, and grange halls at 25¢ a head. Russell's posters proudly billed it as 'three miles long,' though it was actually slightly less than a quarter of a mile. And over eight and a half feet tall. Any question about false advertising is debatable: it certainly must have *seemed* like three miles long to the artists as they laboriously brushed gallon after gallon of paint — most of it blue — onto the canvas.

The depiction was accurate enough that Harvard

historian Samuel Eliot Morison called it "the pictoral counterpart of Melville's great classic *Moby Dick*." It travelled the cities and towns and hamlets entertaining those fortunate enough not to have gone off whaling themselves. It was not the only panorama around: others of the era included *Burning Moscow*, *Down the Mississippi* and *The Battle of Gettysburg*, all competing for the quarters of the populace.

The Purrington & Russell Panorama is especially important to the visual history of Hawai'i because of its 1843 depictions of Lahaina Roadstead on Maui and Kealakekua Bay on the Big Island of Hawai'i.

Russell painted this scene of Hawaiians in outrigger canoes paddling out to barter with an American whaleship anchored in Kealakekua Bay on the Big Island. Some sixty years before, English navigator Captain James Cook lost his life here in a dispute with natives.

Femme des îles Sandwich.

Above and facing page from the Honolulu Academy of Arts

On October 23, 1819, seven Congregationalist missionaries — six with spouses of but a few weeks — clambered aboard the brig *Thaddeus* to begin their rough, cramped, seasick voyage from Boston around the Horn to the Sandwich Isles. They landed, almost five and a half months later, at Kawaihae on the Big Island: seven missionaries, their seven wives (four now pregnant), Daniel Chamberlain's five children, and four Hawaiian youths "saved" in New England to act as translators and go-betweens.

The situation the missionaries anticipated and the one they found on their arrival were vastly different. Their talks in New Haven with Henry Obookiah and the other displaced Hawaiians had taught them of the warrior king, Kamehameha the Great. And it had taught them of the ancient religion, with its many gods, *kapu* (taboos) and human sacrifices, a religion that they hoped to supplant with their own beliefs.

What they actually discovered when they arrived, which they must have surely taken as a Sign from God, was Kamehameha dead almost a year and the ancient religion crumbling, leaving a vacuum awaiting them instead of rejection or death.

Many foreigners already in the Islands were an unsavory lot, having either 'jumped ship' of their own volition or been dumped ashore by disgruntled captains. A few, like Old John Young, the Spaniard Don Marin, and John Palmer Parker, were trusted confidants to the *alii*. The new king, Liholiho, granted the missionaries just one year in which to prove themselves — a task to which they set with great resolve. Within four months, they excommunicated one of their number, Dr. Thomas Holman, because his streak of stubborn independence could not be tolerated by the stern Congregationalist 'family.' They established schools and chapels and withstood the unsettling politics of both overlapping rulers and overcharging traders. Honolulu, in particular, was a town in disarray, already in 1820 a

The lei niho palaoa, lei of the toothed whale, was a symbol of the first born of chiefly families. Niho kohola, the tooth of the whale, represented Kanaloa, the Sustainer. The comings and goings of the great whales were dependable, like the seasons expressing the firm order of the universe. The whale was a great power, unseen but felt. A beached sperm whale provided about fifty teeth which were first carved with specially prepared sandstone tools, then rough-polished with the tip of a marlin's beak and fine-polish with pumice of coral, a paste of slack-lime, and worn sharkskin. Oiling followed. Lei niho palaoa represents through its shape "the tongue of the commander," the power of the divine word. The necklace of eight-braided human hair represents aka, the black cord, the spiritual cord that connects the wearer to the present, future, and past. The Hawaiians also carved other whale ivory images, ki'i palaoa, seen by the missionaries as graven images and destroyed. Very few survive. After Western contact and the arrival of the half-round iron file, production of lei niho palaoa soared in the face of increasing demand from visitors to the islands.

The history of this spectacular Hawaiian feather cape is entwined in royalty, whaling and tragedy. Originally belonging to Kamehameha the Great, it was carried by his son, Liholiho (Kamehameha II) on his 1823 trip to London aboard the English whaler L'Aigle captained by Valentine Starbuck of Nantucket. The cape was made from the red 'i'iwi and yellow 'o'o feathers and features a very unique checkerboard pattern.

King Kamehameha II presented it to Starbuck upon their safe arrival in London, where the royal party would meet tragedy. Both the king and his young queen, Kamamalu, contracted measles, a disease to which they had no resistance, and died in London in the summer of 1824. The "Starbuck Cape" stayed in that family for over a century and was donated in 1927 to Honolulu's Bishop Museum by Evangeline P. Starbuck.

sailor's paradise of grog, gambling and loose women. The newly-arrived missionaries' concept of paradise did not include these particular three features, and they set about eliminating them from Hawai'i as well.

Within two years, the missionaries had unveiled an incredible tool — a bedraggled Rampage printing press and a few fonts of battered type — and set it up in Honolulu under the hand of Elisha Loomis — a printer before joining the First Company. By codifying the Hawaiian language from spoken to written, using twelve letters — five vowels and seven consonants — the missionaries were able to teach thousands of Hawaiians, beginning with the *alii,* to read and write. A second small press was shipped to Lahainaluna Seminary on Maui in 1834, and it was soon as busy as the first. By 1842 — just twenty years after Elisha Loomis had run off his first speller — the two hand presses had produced over one hundred and thirteen *million* printed pages. Hawaiians, adults and children alike, learned to read and write at an astonishing pace. Within a few years the literacy rate of Hawai'i surpassed that of all the 'civilized' nations of the world "except Scotland and New England."

Some ninety missionaries — divided into twelve Companies between 1820 and 1848 — were sent to the Sandwich Isles, although that number is deceiving, as most of them returned home to New England and were subsequently replaced by others. Of the First Company's seven original missionaries, for example, only two — Asa Thurston and Samuel Whitney — spent their lives in Hawai'i. The other five trickled back to New England between 1821 and 1840. That same ratio held pretty much constant throughout the Mission's presence in the Islands.

Most of the missionaries, like most present day Peace Corps volunteers, did their jobs, completed their 'tours,' and went home. A few, like William Richards and Gerrit Judd, came to wield tremendous political influence. Others left the Mission and went into business in the Islands: Samuel Northrup Castle and Amos Starr Cooke started the Big Five company which today still bears their names. And many Mission children and grandchildren became business, political and social scions.

It is ironic that all the problems the missionaries anticipated finding in the Islands — tribal warfare, resistance (or perhaps attack) by kahunas (priests) of the ancient religion, or even outright refusal to allow them to land — simply failed to materialize. And one problem they had not anticipated — the unruly, rambunctious whalers — had come around the Horn from New England just as they had.

The first whaleships ever in Hawaiian waters arrived just a month before the missionaries departed Boston Harbor, and as *Thaddeus* plowed inexorably toward Hawai'i with its bible-thumping passengers, word of the freshly-discovered whaling grounds off Japan spread through the Pacific fleet like wildfire.

Both these groups of New Englanders, the pious mission companies and the raucous whalers, arrived in the Sandwich Isles simultaneously but, of course, with very different goals. The missionaries sorely wanted the Islanders' souls, while the whalers were more than happy to settle for their bodies.

The whalemen wanted Hawaiian bodies of *both* sexes — female, for recreational purposes, and male to replace crewmen who had been lost at sea or had jumped ship. By the 1840s — when whaling in Hawai'i was in full swing — the whaleships had a personnel crisis of monumental proportions.

Above: An 1848 Perkins lithograph of the village of Lahaina, Maui looking down from Lahainaluna. Whaleships are shown at anchor in the Roadstead. The white building is the Seminary and printery.

Laura Jernegan

A Family Touch

*T*he life of a seafaring man's wife was never easy, even when he was gone for a few days or weeks at a time. Communications were non-existent, and sails would disappear over the horizon and never return — the victim of a sudden storm, an enemy man-of-war, an accident, a rogue whale.

As the voyages in search of whales got longer and longer, as months stretched to a year and then to three or four, the life of the wife left behind became ever more difficult. With her husband thousands of nautical miles away, any news from home would be, at best, months old. The whalers set up a make-shift post office in the Galapagos Islands off Ecuador — in a box covered by an enormous tortoise shell. Ships leaving New England would deposit letters there for men already cruising the Pacific, and ships heading for home would carry mail from those still whaling. It was an uncertain system at best: one wife wrote over a hundred letters to her husband. He received six.

The whalers' mail situation improved markedly when Hawai'i became the twice-a-year provisioning stop for whaleships in the Pacific. The news was still old, but now, at least, it usually got there. The basic problem was unchanged, however, since whalers were still separated from their wives for as long as five years.

Then an interesting phenomenon occurred. Some Yankee master's wife insisted one morning upon going along for the voyage, and her undoubtedly astonished husband capitulated. The first whaleship which lumbered out of Nantucket or New Bedford with the captain's wife waving from the starboard rail must have caused no little consternation in the staid, predominantly Quaker whaling community.

But the idea worked! Despite the naysayers and superstitious, the presence of a woman on board the grimy, greasy whaleship had a positive effect on the conditions and crew. By the 1850s, it was not at all

MARCH 6. 1870.

MY DEAR GRANMA.

WE ARE AT SEA NOW. I EXPECT WE
SHAL BE AT HONOLULU IN ONE WEEK.
I HAVE A LITTLE KITTEN. SHE IS
GOOD. SHE IS BLACK AND WHITE.
I CAN WRITE A LITTLE. I AM GOING
TO HAVE A TEASET. PRESCOTT IS
OUT ON DECK. WHERE ARE YOU NOW.
I SHOULD LIKE TO KNOW. WHERE.
I SUPPOSE YOU ARE IN EDGARTOWN.
I AM GOING TO WRITE AUNT EVA A
LETTER. YOU HAVE HAD TO WAIT
A LONG TIME FOR YOUR
LETTER. WE WENT TO AN ISLAND
NAMED OHITAHOO AND STAID
EIGHT DAYS. WE WENT TO THE
QUEENS PALACE, AND SHE MADE
A FEAST FOR US. MAMA WAS
THE FIRST WHITE WOMAN THAT
EVER WAS ON THE ISLAND. WE
HAD TEN DIFFERENT KINDS OF
FRUITES. I WILL NAME THEM.

ORAGES. BANANAAS. PINEAPPLES.
PLANTAINS. BREADFRUIT, COCONUTS.
LEMONS. MUMMIE APPLES. LIMES.
GUAVAS. WE WENT TO ANOTHER
ISLAND NAMED NOUKAHIVA. AND
PRESCOTT AND I HAD A NICE TIME
THE WHITE PEOPLE HERE
ARE ALL FRENCH. WE WENT TO
SEE THE GOVERNOR. AND THE
QUEEN. AND THE SISTERS OF
CHARITY. PAPA HAS TAKEN 4
SPERM WHALES THAT MADE
89 BARRELS. I HAVE HAD A
PRESENT OF A VERY HANDSOME
WRITING DESK. AND A SILVER FRUIT
KNIFE. I HOPE I SHALL HAVE A
LETTER FROM YOU. AND AUNT EVA.
I SEND MY LOVE TO YOU AND
AUNT BINNIE. AND ALL THE REST.
PRESCOTT AND I SEND YOU
LOTS OF KISSES.

FROM YOUR DEAR LAURA.

unusual that the master's wife go on long Pacific voyages. A July 25, 1849 entry in C. W. Morgan's diary reads, "Capt. Prince W. Ewer will probably go again in the *Emily Morgan* and Mrs. Ewer will accompany him. This custom is becoming quite common and no disadvantages have been noticed. There is more decency when a woman is aboard."

And as women went, so too went their children,

Courtesy Yankee Magazine

Two sons of Edgartown whaling masters demonstrate a unique method of making money from the sea that was quicker, more lucrative and closer to shore than their fathers' had been.

off on whaling voyages halfway around the globe. Oftimes these families would stay in Honolulu or Lahaina, especially when the ships were headed for the dangerous Arctic grounds. One such temporary resident of Honolulu seemed to enjoy her stay in Hawai'i immensely: Mrs. Alexander Whelden, wife of the master of the bark *John Howland*, wrote in March of 1868, "I am loth to lay aside my pen, so enraptured am I with the beauty of these islands...All that is purchasable in the capitals of the world is not to be weighed in comparison with the simple enjoyment that may be crowded into one hour of life on these islands of beauty...Soon we shall say good-bye to this flowery bank, this ripple-marked shore, looking no longer upon the white caps of blooming vines, but with moistened eyes turn our gaze to the everchanging white-caps of the restless sea."

One family which often visited Hawai'i was the Jared Jernegans, from Edgartown, on the little island

of Martha's Vineyard. Captain Jernegan came home from one voyage to find his first wife had died. He remarried a few years later and took his new bride, Edgartown schoolteacher Helen Clark, off to sea.

In October 1868, they departed Edgartown in the bark *Roman* with their two small children, Laura and Prescott, who were tutored in formal school lessons by their mother. Laura kept a daily journal of life aboard *Roman* with a boisterous younger brother, a crew of mutinous whalers, and a revolving sequence of pets — some of which became the main course at the captain's table. She also wrote newsy letters to her grandmother back in Edgartown, one of which is shown here, written when she was eight.

A year and a half after this letter was posted, the whaler *Roman*, commanded by Laura's father, was abandoned in the Arctic ice. Captain Jernegan was rescued and was soon offered another ship. He retired in 1888, after sixteen voyages over 48 years.

Laura herself never went on a whaler again. She returned to Edgartown, later married an Engineer in the U.S. Revenue Service and became a well-known local artist. She died in 1947 at age 85.

Younger brother Prescott had a checkered career as an ordained Baptist minister turned scoundrel! In 1896, he prepared a prospectus offering shares in the Electrolytic Marine Salts Company which had, he claimed, found a secret process to extract gold from seawater. What Prescott had actually found was a secret process to extract gold from investors. His stratagem was simple: at the end of a long pier stretching into the Bay of Fundy, Jernegan gathered prospective shareholders for a demonstration of his amazing process. Slowly lowering a large box containing his secret formula down through a hole in the dock, he'd haul it back up full of gold — placed there by his accomplice, one Charles Fisher, who worked the undersea half of the scheme. Gullible investors — often other Baptist clergy or widows of same — signed right up, and the pair collected hundreds of thousands of dollars before disagreeing and fleeing (separately) to Europe. Fisher, incidentally, was also a scion of a famous Edgartown whaling family (whose father is shown in scrimshaw on page 60). Rev. Jernegan lost the last of his stake by investing it all in a British company which claimed to have a secret formula for extracting gold from seawater! Unable to find work, he finally went to the Philippines around the turn of the century and there became a respected educator. He penned a famous popular song, entitled "Philippines, My Philippines" to the tune of "O, Tannenbaum." He later moved to Hawai'i, and was both a teacher and principal of Hilo High School until his retirement in 1924.

Lahaina Whaling Museum

Scrimshaw

"When cruising the day is passed in the most utter idleness... After the decks are thoroughly scrubbed, washed off, and dried, the cook announces breakfast, and with this the day's work is finished...We had looked forward to this period with anticipations of great pleasure. But man tires of nothing so quickly as a state of inactivity, and so we were not a week upon the whaling ground, ere everyone complained of the weary monotony of such a life."

Chas. Nordhoff, 1877

Above: Extracting sperm whale teeth, from the collection of Robert Van Dyke.

A whaling voyage was filled with hours and days and sometimes weeks with nothing to do. Even the sailors' favorite time-killer — lying to one another about their astonishing prowess with the opposite sex — even that, eventually lost its lustre.

Emerging from the boredom was scrimshaw, a true folk art that focused a whaler on materials at hand: sperm whale teeth, whalebone, coconut shells, seashells, exotic tropical woods, tortoise shell, and, when whaling reached the Arctic, walrus tusks.

Ivory became the 'canvas' on which the whalers painted their daydreams, and scrimshaw became their obsession, filling days and weeks. They were called *scrimshanders*, and to a man they knew the joy of finishing a piece, giving it a final polish and tucking it away to be shared at voyage's end.

There are four basic kinds of scrimshaw. First is the traditional engraved ivory tooth or tusk. The extracted tooth was sanded smooth with sharkskin — an abundant supply of which often circled the whaleships, still attached to its original owner.

Once the tooth was made satin smooth, a scene was scratched into the ivory and all the grooves filled with lampblack. Many of these drawings are primitive. These men, after all, were not artists by trade, and they were working with handmade tools on extremely hard surfaces with compound curves. With their ship rolling and pitching beneath them, it is astonishing to see how many beautiful pieces resulted.

The second type of scrimshaw is ivory carved in myriad forms like cane handles, jagging wheels for pie crusts, and clothespins, many highly detailed.

Third is baleen ('whalebone'), sometimes as flat engraved busks for the corsets of the day, but also used for complex mechanical contrivances like expandable swifts for winding yarn.

The fourth type is when different materials are used such as woods, tortoise shell, or silver hammered from coins and combined with whale ivory or bone.

Above right: A delicately carved whale ivory cane handle depicting a very stylishly outfitted lady of the 19th century.
Far right: Engraved sperm whale tooth.

Above and right, Lahaina Whaling Museum

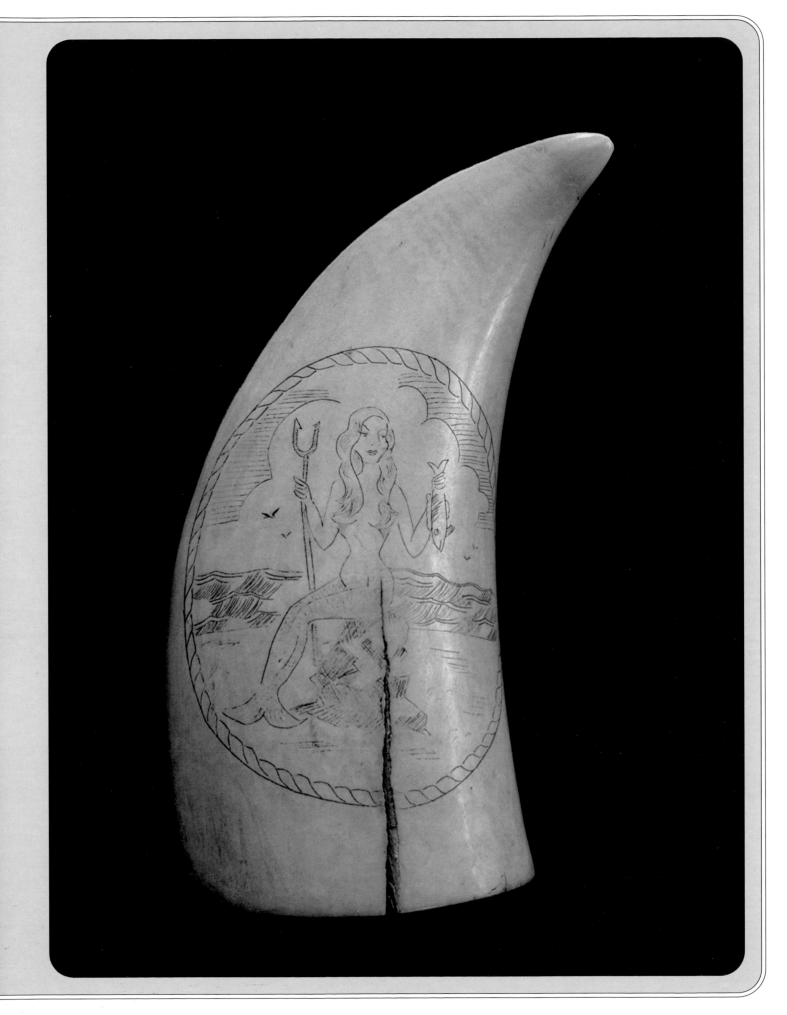

Whalemen would carry their projects around the ship with them, even while on watch or up in the lonely crow's nest on the lookout for whales. This preoccupation with scrimshaw did not necessarily improve their job performance. Famed New Bedford whaling artist Clifford Ashley wrote, "...on occasion Scrimshanders had sighted whales, and rather than be interrupted at a particularly fascinating point in the practice of their Art, had failed to announce them!"

Left and above, Lahaina Whaling Museum

The entry of June 17, 1881 in the diary of harpooneer William Ferguson, a young Scotsman aboard the New Bedford whaler Kathleen, *"...we were off the Island of Juan De Nova on St. Christopher in latitude 17°3'S, longitude 42°47'E. Lots of men are making small ditty boxes and other things of ivory, rosewood or ebony. I am still working on my coconut dipper and have the handle riveted on with silver rivets. Now I must wait until the shell gets hard so that it will take a good polish."*
Left: *An assortment of scrimshaw including fancy cane handles, and two carved whales — a right and a sperm. The large knife has a scrimshawed handle; the smaller one is actually a letter-opener.*

Detail of whalebone busk

Many of the scrimshawed items were for the girl(s) back home, so as a whaleship docked in New Bedford or Nantucket after a four-year absence, the wives and girlfriends of the returning crew would be innundated with trinkets of ivory. One contemporary observer "counted seven brooches myself on Miss Pole's dress," whether from one industrious suitor or seven different ones is not noted.

The laborious effort which went into scrimshaw *is* noted though, in the whalers' own journals and logs. In one instance, Captain Howland of the bark *Kathleen* (sunk, years later, by a whale) took over four months just to carve an ivory paperweight. In another journal, a whaler named William Whitecar wrote, "Every man in the ship had more or less this description of articles; the greater part of which had been constructed aboard from the jaws or teeth of the sperm whales. Our occupation with these things continued...in some instances whole weeks. Thus time glided on, until we found ourselves hurried along by the northeast trades."

Hurried along toward home. There to present Mother with an elaborately carved ivory swift for winding wool and Aunt Janet with a jagging wheel for crimping pie crusts and gouty Uncle Alec with an ivory-handled cane, and who could forget, a brooch or two for the lovely Miss Pole.

Right: A swift was an ultimate challenge for a whaleman artist. Used to wind yarn for knitting, it was designed to expand or contract. Swifts were made from more than one hundred pieces of whalebone and ivory fitted precisely together with silver or brass rivets. This doubleswift has an ivory clamp at its base and a pin cushion crown.

Left and above, Lahaina Whaling Museum

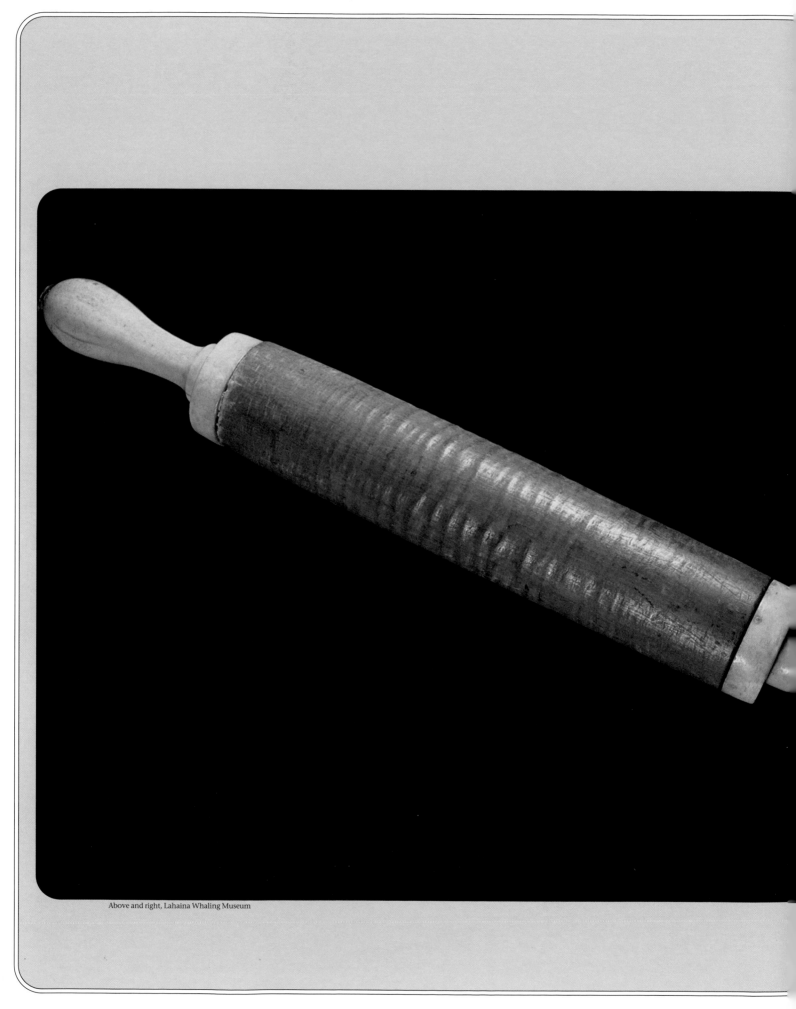

Above and right, Lahaina Whaling Museum

Top: *Engraved whale ivory clothespins.*
Above: *Carved ivory pie crimpers were called 'jagging wheels' and were a popular item among whalers homesick for a fresh-baked cherry pie from the orchards of New England.*
Left: *Tropical-wood rolling pin with whale ivory handles.*

Above and right, Lahaina Whaling Museum

Left: *Busks for his lady's corset. The two outer ones are scrimshawed from a sperm whale's jawbone. The middle one is made of whalebone from the mouth of a baleen whale. The busk was used as a 'stay' to provide reinforcement. One busk bore this inscription:*

> "Accept dear girl this busk from me;
> carved by my humble hand
> I took it from a sperm whale's jaw,
> one thousand miles from land!
> in many a gale has been the whale,
> in which this bone did rest,
> his time is past, his bone at last,
> must now support thy breast."

Far left top: *Captain Charles Fisher of the bark* Alaska, *immortalized here in scrimshaw, is credited with the distinction of capturing the largest sperm whale ever. It was very late in the game — 1884 — so the old bull had likely survived dozens of sightings, chases and attacks. A large sperm whale yielded around a hundred barrels of oil, at 31.5 gallons per barrel. Fisher's immense catch yielded 168 barrels. His son harpooned investors instead of whales and was Rev. Prescott Jernegan's accomplice in the 'gold from seawater' scheme detailed on page 49.*

Far left bottom: *Many toys were made by whalers for family back home or the Captain's children aboard. Very few of these toys have survived, a situation any parent will surely understand. This unusual doll's cradle is made of koa wood with whale ivory inlays.*

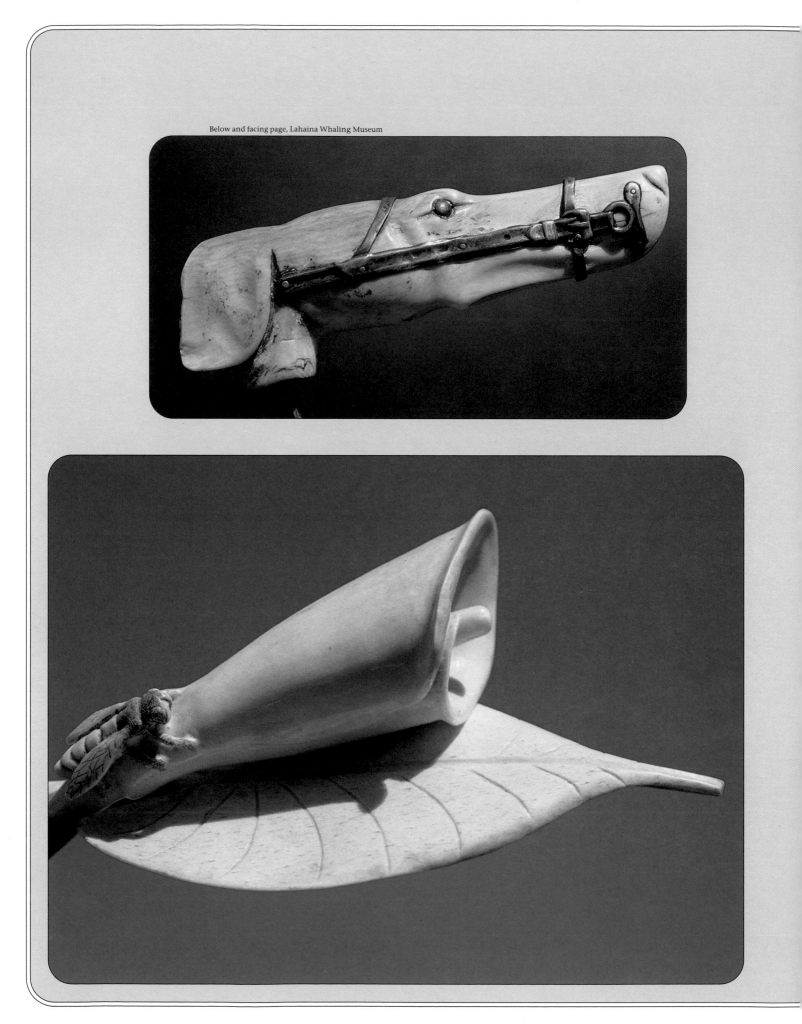

Below and facing page, Lahaina Whaling Museum

Left bottom: This unusual piece of the whaler's folk
art is an intricately detailed carved bee alighting on a lily.
Left top: A rare ivory cane handle carved in the shape
of a whippet's head, with a brass eye and a harness of
silver, probably hammered from coins.
Above: This stylized American eagle was carved as a
cane handle from a sperm whale's tooth. The whalers
fancied themselves distinguished if they went into town
freshly bathed, freshly shaved, with clean clothes from
their sea chest, and sporting a handsome cane.

Right: A rare ivory, bone and wood scrimshawed spool holder descended in the seafaring Kimball family of Waldoboro, Maine. The Kimball family had 13 brothers, all of whom were mariners and it is believed that this unique little stand was made by one of them. The stand is crested with a miniature tower complete with a whale ivory bell, and is supported by three whalebone Queen Anne style feet. Wooden compass rose inlays are in each of its three tiers, and the two larger tiers each have five turned bone spool holders. Nearly a foot in height, the spool holder is from the mid-nineteenth century.

Below: Whalers were not the only ones with time on their hands. During the Napoleanic Wars (1795-1815), thousands of French prisoners languished in British jails where they carved soup bones from the kitchen into creations like this delicately pierced bone sewing box.

65

Below and facing page: Most sperm whale teeth were decorated by simply scratching a design into the ivory with a pointed tool. It was rare for the scrimshander to actually carve high relief. A Scottish whaleman probably carved these images of his ancient Pict ancestors.

Sandwich Islands Banjo

Right: Whalers loved to sing, and they would often bring instruments aboard or make them during a voyage. This unique banjo, with its inlaid scrimshaw "Sandwich Islands" nameplate, is made from the shell of a coconut and, more than likely, the skin of a cat. Probably created and played by one of the many Cape Verde whalers recruited from Portuguese West Africa (now Senegal), it is almost identical to the gourd banjos made there.

Far Right: Many sea-faring songs were rhythmic 'chanteys' sung during heave, heave, heave work like hauling on sail lines or winching up the anchor. The whaling songs, on the other hand, were more like drinking sing-alongs. The Sandwich Islands banjo was almost certainly strummed along to this song, on the way to old Mowee.

Special musical arrangement by Warren Cohen, courtesy of Berkeley F. Fuller

Rollin' Down to Old Mowee

♩ = 120

It's a damn tough life full of toil and strife we whal-in' men un-der go

We don't give a damn when the gale is done, how hard the wind did blow

Our main mast's sprung, Our whal-in's done, and we'll soon be loose and free

We don't give a damn when we've drunk our rum with the girls of old Mow-ee

CHORUS Rollin' down to old Mow-ee my boys, Rollin' down to old Mow-ee --

We're homeward bound from the Arc-tic Ground, Rollin' down to old Mow-ee.

Once more we'll sail with a northernly gale
Through the ice and wind and rain
And those coconut fronds on that tropical land
We soon shall see again.
Six hellish months have passed away
In the cold Tamchatka Sea
And now we're bound from that Arctic Ground
Rollin' down to old Mowee.

CHORUS

How soft the breeze through the Island trees
Now the Ice is far astern
The native maids in their native glades
Are awaiting our return.
Even now their big brown eyes look out
Hoping some fine day to see
Our baggy sails running from the gales
Rollin' down to old Mowee.

CHORUS

The Master and his tools

*T*he title of the man was Captain, but the title of the job was Master, and once at sea all pretense of democracy ceased. Every ship was a floating dictatorship, and the stern tradition of the sea made the Master's word absolute law. Responsibility for the vessel, for the crew, and for success of the voyage rested with this one man.

The American master was unique. Almost every one had worked his way up from the fo'c's'le, and many still steered a boat and lanced the whales. The mates, as well, had not so long before been green hands, and all ship's officers understood their crew.

More often than not, the master served as "ship's doctor" as well, equipped with simple remedies like tincture of iodine, administered either internally or externally, epsom salts and rations of brandy. For the more seriously afflicted, he could clear the charts off his table and use his cabin as an operating theatre, setting broken bones as best he could and amputating whatever seemed unmendable.

All in all, the master's tools were limited but effective. The technology seems simple — canvas and rope, compass and spyglass, octant and charts — yet an experienced master could use these to guide his ship and his crew safely (and profitably) through the stormy and reef-strewn oceans of the world.

Left: Master's spy-glasses, brass-tubed, leather-wrapped and collapsible refracting telescopes. The double convex lenses were ground and polished by hand and provided a magnification of between eight and twenty power.
Right: Portrait of Captain Rotch, a frequent visitor to the Sandwich Islands, who sailed out of Fair Haven, Mass.

Above and facing page, Lahaina Whaling Museum

The octant was a predecessor to the sextant still used today for navigation. Both determine a ship's latitude by measuring the height of the sun above the horizon at high noon. The technique was called "shooting the sun" and a red or green glass filter protected the eye from the sun's reflection in the octant's mirror.

A Hadley's octant from the collection of the Lahaina Whaling Museum

Day by Day by Day

*O*ften kept by the first mate, a whaleship log was a daily chronicle of position coordinates, weather, whales sighted, landfalls, and the happenings aboard. Taciturn or loquacious, over a lengthy voyage each logbook's style accurately reflected its keeper's personality.

The log pictured is from the collection of the Lahaina Whaling Museum and covers a voyage in 1852 of the bark *Clara Bell* from the little seacoast town of Mattapoiset, just north of New Bedford.

The thousands of whaling log books were so detailed about landfalls, harbors, currents, tides and reefs, that the U.S. Navy utilized them during the early days of World War II. The logs profiled the islands and atolls of the Pacific — like Tarawa, Eniwetok, and Guadalcanal — which the Navy would soon be attacking, defending, or using as supply dumps or air strips.

This information was, for a time, all the Navy had — a belated legacy from the Yankee whalers, who had, a century or so before, "whitened the Pacific with their canvas" in search of the Leviathans.

A

JOURNAL

OF A

WHALING. VOYAGE

PERFORMED

IN

BARK. CLARA. BELL

OF

MATTAPOISETT.

DANIEL.FLANDERS.

MASTER

COMMENCING

AUGUST. 7.th 1852.

Sat Aug 7. 1852

Light winds and fine weather
at 7 A.M. got underway and stood
out of the harbour

Sunday Aug. 8

Light winds from S.W. beating
out of the bay at midnight
came to anchor in Chamunsha
bight with best bower in 8 fathoms water with
45 fathoms chain. Latter part
light winds and good weather

Monday Aug 9

Light winds from S.W.
Still lying at anchor in the bight
at 5 P.M. had religious meeting
on board. about 400 on board
closed at sunset. Latter part
pleasant & light winds from S.W.
8 A.M. Got under way and stood
to sea

Tuesday 10

Light winds from S.W. beating
out the sound at 1 P.M. discharged
pilot. at 6 P.M. No mans land bore
N P.W. 10 miles distant. Stowed our
anchors. Middle & latter part same
employed in fitting boats.

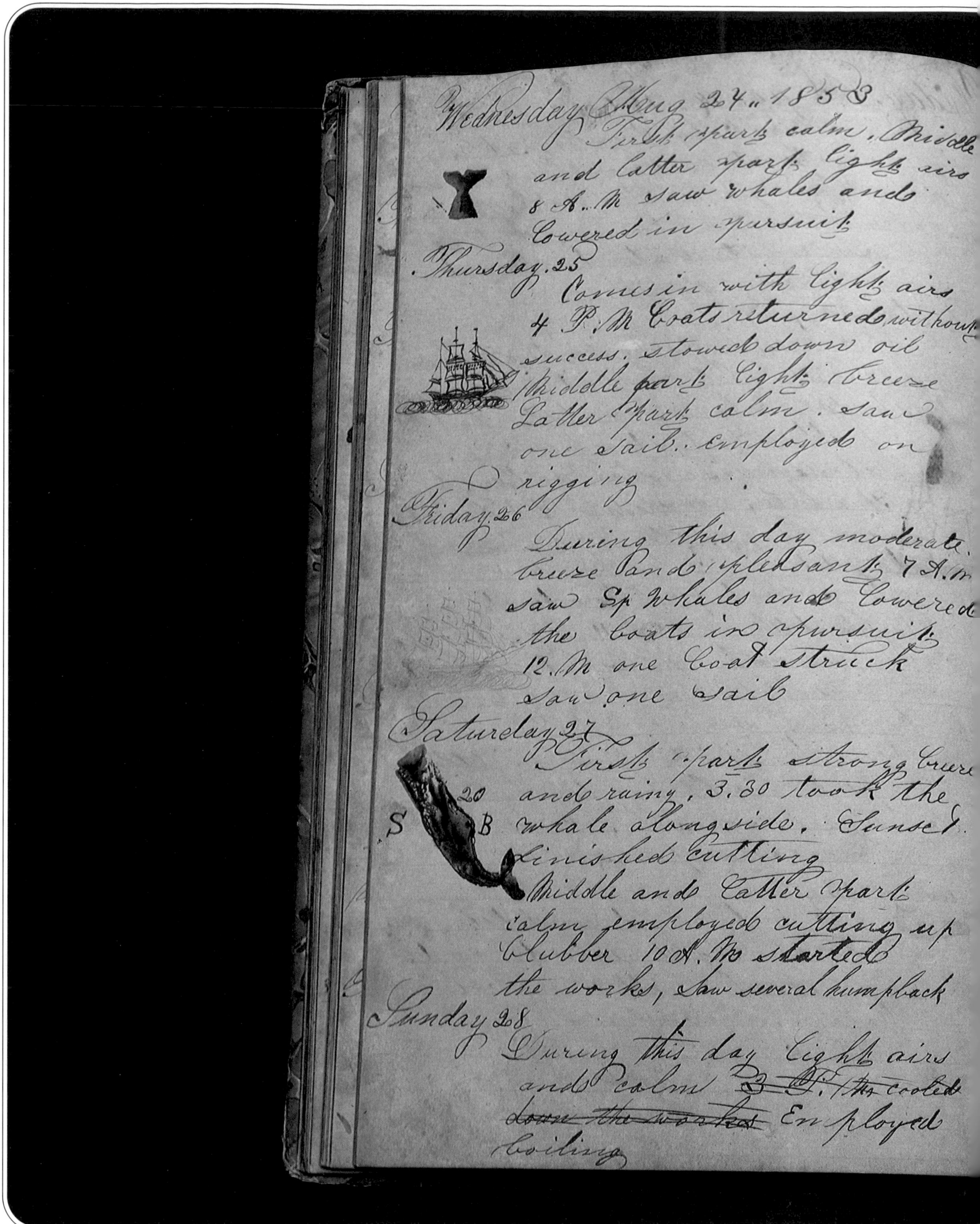

Wednesday Aug 24" 1858
First part calm. Middle
and latter part light airs
8 A. M saw whales and
lowered in pursuit

Thursday 25
Comes in with light airs
4 P. M Boats returned without
success. Stowed down oil
Middle part light breeze
Latter part calm. Saw
one Sail. Employed on
rigging

Friday 26
During this day moderate
breeze and pleasant 7 A. m
saw Sp whales and lowered
the boats in pursuit
12. M one boat struck
Saw one Sail

Saturday 27
First part strong breeze
and rainy. 3. 30 took the
whale alongside. Sunset
finished cutting
Middle and latter part
calm employed cutting up
blubber 10 A. M started
the works, Saw several humpback

Sunday 28
During this day light airs
and calm 3 P. M cooled
down the works Employed
boiling

Monday Aug 29: 1853 3 P.M cooled down
During this day calm. Saw
white water several times,
Steering to N.E to stem the current.

Tuesday 30 First part moderate breeze
Middle part calm and
squally. Latter part strong
breeze, Steering to Eastward
Saw Black fish

Wednesday 31 First part strong breeze
working to Eastward
Middle part strong breeze and
squally. Latter part strong breeze
saw several breaches and one Sail

Thursday Sept 1 First part strong breeze
Middle and latter parts moderate
breeze working to S.E. Employed
on rigging. Saw one Finback

Friday 2 First part moderate breeze
and pleasant, Middle and
Latter parts moderate breeze
and Squalls of rain. Saw
Black white water.
took a Porpoise. Employed
on rigging

77

Whaling Crews

From the print collection of the Lahaina Whaling Museum

The whaling industry attracted a mixture of the ambitious, the adventurous, the escapist, the eccentric — all heaped together in a tiny, floating space for endless stretches of time — hemmed in on the one side by boredom and on the other by peril. The concoction was, often as not, explosive.

Short of defending the Alamo, there were few jobs in the 1800s worse than crewing on a whaler. The very early off-shore voyages, of a few weeks or so, were not that bad. They were dangerous and dirty, of course, but then so were many other employment opportunities of that era. Setting out in small boats after a whale was also thrilling, and precious few other jobs offered that. Besides, these early whaling crews were composed primarily of neighbors and blood relatives — men whose families had been New England fishermen for the several generations that they had been in the New World. The harpooneers were often Algonquin Indians from the Wampanoag tribe, whose families had been New England fishermen for centuries before that.

As whaling expanded, the first additions to the crews were rawboned farmboys enticed from the hill farms of New Hampshire, Vermont and Maine. They were cajoled into service with tales of excitement and camraderie: two elements sadly lacking on a farm where backbreaking efforts often seemed only to produce an annual crop of fresh granite.

Blacks were the next to be recruited. As whalers worked the coast of Africa, they would sign on black crewmen from the Cape Verde area of Portuguese West Africa (now Senegal). At a time in our history when African blacks were being sold into slavery, the whalers were hiring them on as equal members of the crew. They often worked their way up to mate, and occasionally, master.

As more and more men were needed (it has been estimated that some 40,000 put to sea from New England ports), a crew became an eclectic jumble assembled by an unscrupulous "Shipping Agent" hired to outfit a ship with warm bodies. The lure of

THE CHASE.

free land in the West and then in 1849, GOLD! made it harder and harder to attract crews of quality, and it was not uncommon for some poor devil on a bender in New Bedford to wake up, nursing a monumental hangover, in a rock-hard bunk headed for the far reaches of the Pacific.

A popular saying around New England wharves was, "One voyage on a whaleship is one too many," and the rate of one-timers was much higher than for other types of vessels. Once aboard, the reality often outweighed the romance, and for many, one voyage *was* plenty. For others, just *part* of one voyage was plenty, and they jumped ship at the first opportunity. A young seaman named Herman Melville — much later to become famous as the author of *Moby Dick* — wrote his first book, *Typee*, about his experiences with natives after jumping ship in the Marquesas.

Other men, however, considered whaling their career, and for them, advancement was rapid. Unlike the regimented English crews, which were severely disciplined and class-driven, the Yankees awarded competence and loyalty with promotions. Most of the officers had started on the lowest rung and one, William M. Davis, wrote, "I went to sea as a cabin-boy ten years of age; at fourteen I steered a boat and stuck my first whale; at sixteen I was second mate. I was a boy who meant to be captain or go under, and didn't mean to go under if I could help it. At twenty-two I was master."

Opportunity or no, the life aboard a whaleship was godawful. The vessel itself wallowed through the seas like a floating bathtub, which it resembled somewhat. Top speed was a leisurely five knots, for there was no real rush in cruising the whaling grounds, such as there was for the sleek, sail-heavy clippers racing cargos back and forth in trade. The whaleships were cramped, vermin-infested, and reeked of death. Most of a voyage was tediously uneventful, and the intricately carved and engraved scrimshaw was one result of long hours with nothing else to do.

The excited cry *"Thar she blows!"* from the lookout perched perilously in the crow's nest high on the swaying mainmast, always broke that tedium. Every whaleship had some four or five sleek whaleboats, jampacked with gear and always ready to go, suspended out over the ocean on curved davits. At least two boats were lowered immediately as their crew — like firemen on a brass pole — slid down the lines and scrambled for their stations. The next hours were often terrifying, and always hard work.

Once in the water, stealth was all-important. Oarlocks were padded and greased, often sheathed in leather, as whales seemed to learn quickly that the fellows in the boat had less than friendly intentions. Later whaleboats carried an easily-hoisted mast and jib, so they could scud silently toward the Leviathan like deadly day sailors. The whaleboats also carried paddles and could be silently propelled canoe-style, but apparently this was not often done.

Normally — from the drawings and descriptions which have come down to us — the whaleboats were rowed, with a steady cadence from the mate at the tiller. As they closed on the whale, the sail — if it was up — was lowered, and the harpooneer would leave his seat and climb over the tightly-packed equipment towards the prow of the boat.

Wedging his 'larboard' (left) knee into a clumsy cleat notched out for just that purpose, he would heft the long harpoon in his calloused hand, poised for the throw. As the whaleboat maneuvered close, he would thrust the harpoon deeply into the Leviathan's flank, and if there was time, he would plant a second one, attached to the whaleline with a loop, in case the first 'iron' came loose. As the harpoon sliced into the whale's thick blubber, the mate manning the steering oar would holler, "Astern all!," and the crew would strain mightily against their long oars to distance themselves and their frail craft away from their wounded (and surprised) prey.

This was a dangerous time, for as the whale reacted to the hit, he might well smash the fragile craft with his tail or seize it in his jaws. These were not common occurrences, but they did happen, and were extra incentive to pull hard on the oars.

LOWERING THE BOATS.

The Whaleboat

*T*he whalers' instrument of death was not so much the lance, as the whaleboat. A sleek 'double-ended' craft, fragile but strong, the whaleboat could be sailed, rowed or paddled towards its prey — whether that prey be an 60-ton sperm whale near the Equator or some young ladies in Lahaina.

Whaleboats were between 28' and 30' in length, carried a crew of six, and were extremely sea-worthy craft, crammed with specialized paraphernalia of the trade: harpoons, lances, paddles, oars, linetubs — and a lantern keg of emergency gear, just in case. Both that emergency gear and their sea-worthiness came into play after the whaleship *Essex* was stove in by a sperm whale in 1820, and eight men survived an ordeal of more than 4500 miles and three months at sea, an event which inspire Herman Melville's *Moby Dick*.

The whaleboat was honed to perfection in the seaport boatyards of New England and changed hardly at all in basic design over almost a century and a half. It was relatively inexpensive, easily repairable by the ship's carpenter, and considered expendable.

Around 1850 a centerboard was added, and with it a simple sail — making it easier to sidle up to the increasingly wary whales. This sail was utilized extensively in the Arctic, and the framing of the whaleboat was reinforced for use in the ice there as well. Perhaps the whaleboat's most astonishing feat was the safe carriage of over 1200 souls in hundreds of boats from the icebound Arctic fleet in 1871.

Greener's Gun

The deadly Greener's harpoon gun was invented in the 1840s and manufactured by W.W. Greener in Birmingham, England. Both English and American whalers used it in the Pacific. Mounted on the prow of a whaleboat, a Greener's gun was especially useful in smooth seas. Fully loaded with its four and a half foot harpoon, it weighed 75 pounds and had a maximum range of 84 yards, though the crew would usually try to maneuver closer for more accuracy.

The Greener's gun is a muzzle-loader, fired with double percussion caps struck by its massive hammer. This rare 1874 lithograph from the Lahaina Whaling Museuum by naturalist Charles M. Scammon shows the gun in use.

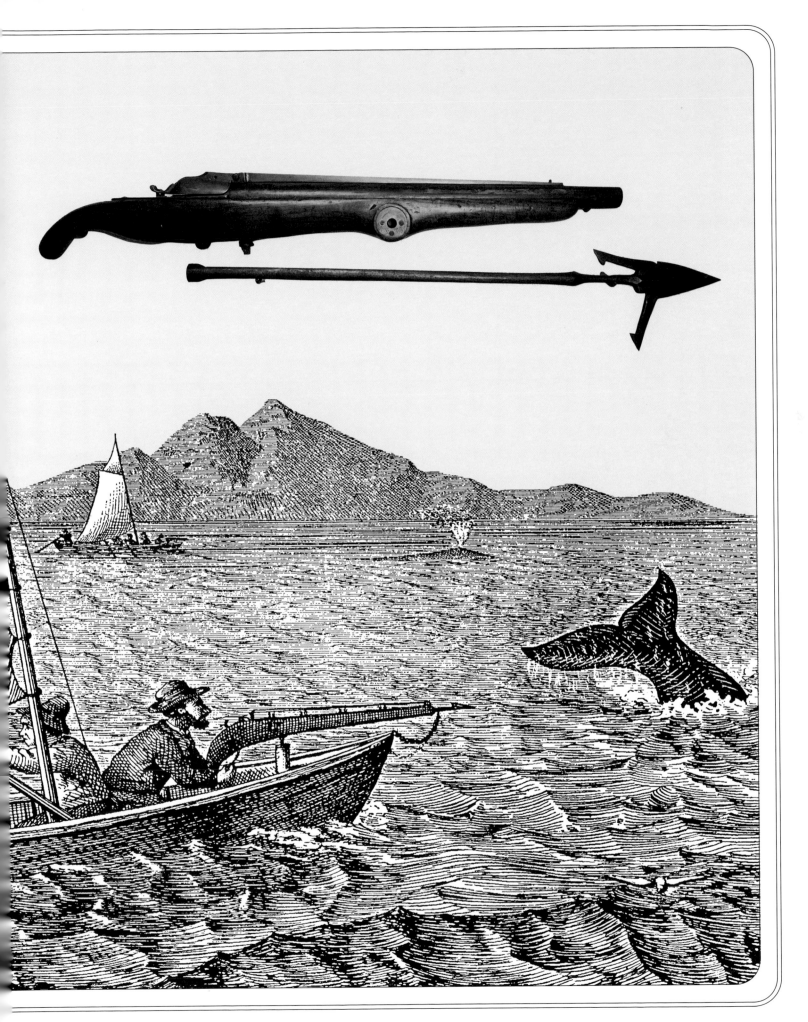

LAYING ON.

The harpooned whale would usually do one of two things: he would run or he would 'sound.' If he ran, the whaleline, of finest quality lightly-tarred hemp, would play out of the tub where it had been carefully coiled. From the tub, the line went back around a post ('loggerhead') in the stern, and then doubled back the length of the boat and out through a chock at the bow. The line would spin round the loggerhead with such speed that it had to be doused with seawater to keep from igniting.

On occasion, a man would literally disappear forever from the whaleboat — snatched from his thwart by the line snagging an arm or leg as it whipped by. Melville described the danger: "When the line is darting out, to be seated then in the boat is like being seated in the midst of the manifold whizzings of a steam-engine in full play, when every flying beam and shaft and wheel is grazing you."

By tradition, the harpooneer in the bow and the mate in the stern would change places, scrambling over the flying line to their new stations. The mate would don thick leather mitts called 'nippers' and try to slow the line down a bit, as the boat careened through the waves on a 'Nantucket Sleigh Ride' at speeds of up to twelve knots. This tow lasted until the whale tired (that once took over eight hours), and then the men could haul themselves alongside their prey for the final kill. The mate would aim his sharp-tipped lance — as best he could in a rocking boat — for the great beast's heart or lungs. Fatally struck, the whale would go into its 'flurry' and spout blood (the 'red flag'), then swim in ever-decreasing circles and roll over on its side, dead.

If the whale had sounded — headed for the depths instead of *away from* the boat — the line would still play out of the tub at tremendous speed, but the boat itself wouldn't go much of anywhere. Each whaleboat normally carried about 300 fathoms of hemp line in a tub — that's more than a quarter-mile — and the crew would have to hastily splice (or 'bend on') the line from their second tub if it looked as if the whale was going even deeper.

Sperm whales have often been called 'natural submarines,' as research scientists have tracked them on sonar diving at least two miles. If the sounding whale went deeper than the amount of line on board, the mate would leap to cut it with a hatchet or knife, rather than risk losing the boat. At least two whaleboats were dragged beneath the sea and lost: one from the *Mars* in 1843 and another, twelve years later, off the *Monticello*. That wasn't common, and usually as soon as the whale surfaced for air, the boat would move in for the kill.

Lots of things could go wrong in this scenario, and in fact often did. "Beware of the right whale's flukes and the sperm whale's teeth," an old saying went. Whaleboats were stove in, and men were lost overboard, or were maimed or killed in dozens of ways. Whaling was a dangerous game: approaching a 60' bull sperm whale weighing 'a ton a foot' in a 28' cedar rowboat was not for the faint of heart.

Killing him was just the beginning. The hard work began when his 'flurry' ended. For the whaleship was far more than a hunter, she was a factory too, and the job of rendering this gigantic creature of the deep into marketable products now began.

Like right whales, one of the advantages of a sperm whale was that it floated when dead. (Many whale species were never hunted until recently, because once they died, they sank like a rock.) The floating whale was towed to the ship by six men in a rowboat, brought up along the starboard side and made fast, with the head towards the stern. A platform called the 'cutting stage' was lowered over the floating whale, and the crew began to remove the head and, simultaneously, slice the blubber.

The head, with its large case of spermaceti and lower jaw filled with ivory teeth, was either wrested on deck or, if it was too large, hoisted up as high as possible to ladle out the spermaceti and slice off the jaw. The body, meanwhile, was being stripped of its insulating blubber by tugging it with an iron hook, block-and-tackled to a mast. These big 'blankets' of blubber were dropped through an open gangway to the blubber room on the deck below, where they were cut into smaller 'horse pieces' and sliced into thin slivers ('bible leaves') to melt more easily in the try-pots back up on deck.

THE FLURRY.

CUTTING IN.

Try-pots were mounted amidships, on a brick and mortar base called the 'caraboose,' which was filled with seawater to insulate the wooden decking below from the heat of the tryworks' fires. These would blaze night and day until they had reduced each whale's blubber to casks of oil — casks built right on deck by the cooper, to fit every nook and cranny of the ship's hold. A huge bull sperm whale would yield more than three thousand gallons of sperm oil and another five hundred of spermaceti. The lower jaw would surrender some fifty ivory teeth, which the second mate would distribute later on for scrimshawing. The real prize — and only a few sperm whales had it — was ambergris, a compacted lump of material found in the large intestine and used in perfume. The price for ambergris ranged up to $15 an ounce — at a time when gold was worth $16 an ounce! The largest chunk ever found weighed well over a thousand pounds.

Reducing each whale to its lowest common denominator, oil, went on day and night. A whaleship which had lucked into a herd of whales, and gotten more than one, just had to keep going, turning their catch into oil before the ever-present sharks, attracted by the blood and the commotion, turned that same catch into dinner. Chasing and killing whales, then processing them "right on the spot" was grim, dirty work, fraught with danger. And it was work performed by men thousands of miles from home, living in conditions so primitive that one whaler, in his memoirs, compared them, quite unfavorably, to pigsties back home in Kentucky.

A whaleship generally carried a crew of close to thirty men. That very same vessel, if switched into service to haul cargo, would carry six to eight. In other words, just sailing the ship from Point A to Point B required the labors of perhaps eight sailors — the rest were on board simply because she was a whaler. 'Close quarters' was an understatement.

And a whaleship was slathered in filth. The sails were smudged a mottled black from the tryworks' smoky fires. The decks were slimy from the blood and the whale oil in which they were often awash. Cockroaches and rodents were everywhere, and whaleships and crew had a certain 'air' about them, especially from downwind.

Adapted from an 1839 linoleum block print by L.L.Balcom, from the Leo J. Chamberlain Collection

Most of the crew, perhaps twenty men, lived together in the forecastle, or fo'c's'le. This room's shape followed the triangle of the bow, and it was tiny, cramped, and dirty, with a ceiling barely five feet above the deck. Crude bunks were nailed in two rows along the hull timbers. The eternally damp fo'c's'le was frigid in winter and sweltering in summer. Ventilation was through a small hatch, usually closed. This fetid room was home for some four years to a varied assortment of whalers of all sizes, shapes and personality defects. The men were crammed together in this smoky, smelly hellhole filled with their sea chests, on which they sat to talk, scrimshaw and eat. Conditions being what they were below, whalemen were topside as much as weather allowed.

Food was a constant source of complaint. The owners had fine-tuned their overhead by alloting just a few cents a day to feed each man! The basic diet was salt pork or salt beef, with hard tack and coffee, three times a day. Floating the hard tack in the coffee until the maggots crawled out and could be skimmed off was a common practice. Despite what might be

Below: Cast iron try-pots held about 250 gallons of boiling oil and had flat sides to fit closer together in the cramped space on deck. As the whaleship headed home, the oil-soaked bricks were tossed overboard.

Lahaina Whaling Museum

TRYING OUT.

Lahaina Whaling Museum

termed a 'plentiful' supply, the taste of whalemeat is so strong that hardly anyone on a whaleship ever ate it. To vary their diet, they would drop anchor occasionally at Pacific islands and trade for fresh fruits, vegetables and meat. And whalers would often stop at the Galapagos Islands off Chile for giant tortoises, which they would stack — upside-down on their shells — in the ship's hold. The turtles could live a year without food or water.

Discipline aboard a whaler was tight — at least in the working periods of hunting and trying whales. There was plenty of free time, and because there was no concern with top speed, men were not constantly scrambling up and down the rigging to adjust sails for that little bit of extra efficiency, as they were on a merchantman. Most of the crew on a whaleship were essentially laborers, not sailors.

There were few mutinies on whalers, but a high desertion rate. Men jumped ship at the drop of a hat — especially in Hawai'i, where they could easily intergrate into an ever-increasing population of non-Hawaiians. But men jumped ship wherever there was land, just to get off that godawful whaler. Herman Melville went over the side of *Acushnet* in the Marquesas and escaped search parties by heading into the mountains to take his chances with the fierce Taipi tribe, long reputed to be cannibals.

After a year aboard a whaler, Melville preferred the unknown to the known. He soon tired of life with the natives and escaped again, this time to sea aboard another whaler, the *Lucy Ann*. He was put ashore in Tahiti as a 'mutineer' and signed on with the *Charles and Henry* to go just as far as Lahaina, where Melville arrived in May 1843 with twenty dollars cash and the clothes on his back. In a few days he was off to Honolulu, where he remained for four months working as a pin-setter in a downtown bowling alley. He was through with whaling forever and returned to the East Coast aboard the warship *United States*. Melville's brief experiences in the Pacific were so intense that he would write about them for the remaining forty-odd years of his life.

Herman Melville was the most articulate of the thousands of men who 'went awhaling' and found it terrible. As voyages got longer and longer, odds of keeping a crew together became ever shorter. Charles Nordhoff wrote, "Not one whaleship in fifty brings home from a three years' cruise the crew which took her out. Few young men are satisfied with the monotonous life of the whaleman, and few of those who complete the voyage...do so not from choice, but because the vigilance of the captain, or their own ignorance of resources...rendered escape impossible... Desperate expedients are sometimes adopted. The greater part of a whaleship crew once drifted to shore on the cover of the tryworks."

The harder it became to fill the forecastle, the lower the standards of employment dipped, and one Nantucket whaleship owner referred kindly to his crew as "pirates and murderers." The missionaries, never at a loss for hyperbole, agreed. Sheldon Dibble of the Fourth Company called whalers "the lowest and most reckless of seafaring men."

Above: A rare photograph of a bailer pouring boiling whale oil into a cooling pot alongside the tryworks.

Hunter, Factory, Warehouse, Home...

A whaleship performed four functions — three of them well. This artist's cutaway view of the *Viola* displays all four graphically. Already successful as a hunter, her sleek whaleboats again hang from their davits out over the sea, ready for another chase.

The crew has set up the ship as a factory, and are dismantling a sperm whale and reducing it to casks of oil and some teeth. Mates with long, razor-sharp spades stand upon the cutting-stage, a hinged platform lowered over the whale to make stripping off the thick layer of blubber easier.

Working above an ocean aswarm with sharks, some mates lashed themselves to the ship to avoid toppling in. Using a large iron hook suspended from the mast, the blubber is peeled from the whale in large 'blanket pieces,' which are lowered through a hatch into the blubber room below. There they are sliced into smaller chunks ('horse pieces') and finally into thin pages, called 'bible leaves' by the irreverent whalers. These are passed topside to be rendered into oil in the try-pots. After cooling, the oil is poured in new oak casks made to size on deck by the cooper, then stored in the whaleship's warehouse, the holds below deck. As a hunter, factory, and warehouse, the whaleship was superb, but as a home she was sadly lacking. Living quarters on the lower deck are, left to right: the captain's spartan stateroom in the stern, the mate's smaller cabins, the harpooneers' and cooper's quarters in steerage amidships, and the crew's rude accomodations in the forecastle.

This cutaway was drawn by Crazy Shirts' graphic designer Derek Mau from the whaleship model Viola.

The Kutusoff

THE SHIP KUTUSOFF SPERM WHALING.

On a bone-chilling November day in the year 1841, the whaler *Kutusoff,* captained by William H. Cox, loosed her moorings in New Bedford Harbor and set sail for the Pacific whaling grounds. On board was a neophyte whaler by the name of Benjamin Russell, a 37 year-old self-taught artist determined to make this voyage a profitable one.

Russell had an idea that New Englanders, proud of their whaling industry, would be willing to pay to experience a whaling voyage vicariously. From the day the *Kutusoff* sailed from New Bedford to the day she returned, three and a half years later, Russell painted, sketched and took notes for his dream, a Whaling Panorama. (See pages 40-41 and 96-97)

He had signed on as an apprentice cooper, to help make the oak casks that held the whale oil. His 'lay' was 1/100 of the ship's profit at voyage end. When the *Kutusoff* arrived back in New Bedford in March 1845, her cargo of oil and bone sold for $89,451 profit. Russell's share of that came to precisely $894.51, but he had accumulated debts — advances and items from the ships store — of the same amount, and he arrived in New Bedford "dead horse" broke.

He debarked the whaler with only his sketches, his notes and his experiences, all of which would enable Russell to soon become the premier artist of the Yankee whaling adventure.

The painting to the left, titled "The Ship *Kutusoff* Sperm Whaling," is an original watercolor which Russell presented to Captain Cox, in whose family it has remained ever since. It now hangs in Honolulu above the desk of Cox's great-great-granddaughter, Pacific historian Rhoda E.A. Hackler, with whose kind permission it is reproduced here.

The painting shows all phases of whaling from the chase to the trying out of the blubber. The *Kutusoff* is shown 'port-painted,' an early form of camouflage. Whaleships were lightly-armed, if they were armed at all, and on occasion had been boarded and seized by hostile South Pacific islanders. Portpainting refers to the common practice of painting fake gunport doors along the hull to frighten the natives into thinking cannon were on board.

Hawai'i Calls

New Bedford Whaling Museum

*O*nce ashore in the Islands, the whalemen, whom missionary Dibble had dubbed "most reckless," often ran wild. The 'saints on earth' were duly outraged by this behavior and filled their somewhat acerbic journals and letters back home with eminently quotable lines like "the floodgates of licentiousness have been opened" and Rev. Henry Cheever's famous description of the Lahaina of the whalers as "one of the breathing holes of Hell."

But missionaries or no missionaries, the whaling enterprise was an economic force of awesome proportions in these Islands for more than forty years. From

Tropical breezes, warm willing ladies, strong drink by the bellyful — these were the dreams of men long at sea. Hawai'i provided all three, and once ashore, the whalers reveled in their new-found freedom. They especially resented the meddlesome missionaries, who beheld themselves "saints on earth."

1820 into the 1860s, the whaling grounds of the North Pacific provided oil for the lamps of the world and lubrication for the machines of industry. Whaleships would visit Hawai'i twice a year, to restock their provisions, trans-ship their oil and whalebone, and give their delirious crews respite. Both Lahaina and Honolulu prospered as never before, as millions of dollars were freely thrust into the economy. The earlier trade in sandalwood enriched a few Yankee traders and a few Hawaiian chiefs. But whaling was different, as it was the first capitalistic venture which truly involved the Hawaiian people.

"A Cluster of Whaleships Refreshing at Lahaina Roadstead" from the 1843 Russell-Purlington Panorama. The large building in the right foreground is the coral palace Hale Piula (literally, iron roof house), which was damaged by high winds in 1858 and subsequently dismantled to use the blocks for the courthouse. The steepled building on the hill behind town is Lahainaluna Seminary.

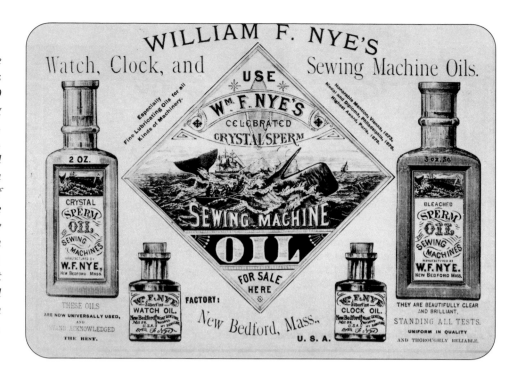

Right: A large sperm whale might yield some 3,000 gallons of sperm oil, or some 192,000 little bottles of Mr. Nye's Sewing Watch and Clock Oil.
Below: In the mid-1850s, Paul Emmert, an artist and printer team, collaborated on a series of twelve lithographs of Honolulu. This 1857 scene shows the newly-chartered city as seen from the harbor, with whaleships at anchor, Honolulu Iron Works at the extreme left, and Nuʻuanu Valley in the left background.

The number of whaleships visiting Hawaiʻi just plain exploded after 1820 as word of the new North Pacific hunting grounds off Japan spread through the fleet. In November 1820, Captain Joseph Allen of the Nantucket whaler *Maro* was the first to arrive back — his holds full of sperm oil — and the rush to the Sea of Japan was on.

Soon, some fifty whaleships were visiting the Sandwich Isles twice a year: in the Spring before setting off to hunt in the waters around Japan, and again in the Fall before going south to cruise the Equator. The vast majority stopped to refit at either Honolulu on Oahu or Lahaina on Maui. Both towns were on the drier leeward shores, yet both had plenty of sweet fresh water to fill the whaleships' casks. The two harbors were (and still are) very different. Honolulu offers a classic deep draught harbor, while Lahaina has a sheltered offshore anchorage called a Roadstead. Honolulu had both shipyard facilities and higher prices, and Lahaina proved to be much more popular. For a time in the middle of the 19th century, little Lahaina was the whaling capital of the world.

Both Lahaina and Honolulu suffered from the push-pull between missionaries and whalers, often precipitated by English sailors, who were even more unrestrained on shore than their Yankee counterparts. The missionaries' influence over certain royalty — especially Hoapili, the governor of Maui — caused much of the whalers' unrest. In October 1825, crewmen from the English whaleship *Daniel* protested a newly-enacted law banning women from visiting the fleet anchored offshore by terrorizing the populace of

Lahaina for three days. They twice threatened the life of Rev. William Richards, whom they had assumed, quite correctly, instigated the law. The whalers were driven off once by sympathetic (and presumably large) Hawaiians and a second time by Richards' feisty young wife.

Two years later another English whaler, the *John Palmer,* this one with a cannon on deck, chafed at the same law and the same missionary. They lobbed a couple of cannonballs of protest into the Mission House, although missing their targeted clergyman.

Despite the good Reverend's efforts, Lahaina remained the whalers' favorite port, as well as a wide open one. Rum-laced 'grog' was prohibited, though beer halls prospered. One infamous concoction invented to circumvent occasional temperance laws was "spruce beer," whose mouth-watering ingredients included tobacco, potatoes and a natural anesthetic, 'awa root. Prostitution was outlawed, but not very

effectively, as both supply and demand far exceeded enforcement efforts. Beginning in the 1820s, both Lahaina and Honolulu continued to attract more and more whalers and more and more businesses. In 1842, Sir George Simpson wrote, "Honolulu presented a strange admixture of the savage and the civilized, stacks of warehouses rising around straw huts."

Companies sprang up, which exist to this day, to supply the whalers and ancillary businesses. Four of the so-called Big Five firms began as merchants and purveyors in the 1800s. C. Brewer was the first, and it is considered the oldest corporation west of the Mississippi — founded in 1826 by the Boston trader James Hunnewell (and named for a later partner, Charles Brewer). The company we know today as Amfac was established in 1849 as a ship chandlery and general agent by German immigrant H. Hackfeld. Two years later, Castle & Cooke was started by a pair of former missionary secular agents, Mssrs. Castle & Cooke.

Collection of Robert E. Van Dyke

HAWAIIAN
SHIPPING ART

We, whose names are hereunto affixed, do hereby agree and bind ourselves to serve in the capacities set opposite our respective names, on board the *Ship* called the *Jamucane* of *New Bedb* whereof *Winslow* is at present Master, now lying in the Port of *Lahaina* and bound to *on a whaling cruise*

for a term of time not to exceed *twelve* months, or until the said *Ship* shall return to these Hawaiian Islands, provided that takes place before the expiration of said term of *12* months. And we further agree, that during said voyage we will perform our duty faithfully, whether on board said *Ship* or in her boats, whether by night or day, as good and obedient seamen. It is also agreed by the Master of said *Ship* that at the end of the voyage, we shall each of us be paid the amount of compensation per month set opposite our respective names in the column marked "Wages." In witness of which agreement, the Master hath hereto first set his name. And we bind ourselves to be on board said vessel at or before the hour of   on the   day of   A. D. 18*56*.

O Makou ka poe i kakau i ko makou iho e hana i ka oihana i k no e waiho ana no ma ke awa o

aole nae e oi aku na malama pae Aina o Hawaii nei; ina paha c Ke ae aku nei no hoi makou, ma ia o ua moku la kai a hoolohe. Ua aeia mai hoi c holo ana, alaila, e hookaaia inai i h o ko makou mau inoa ma ka lalan ka inoa o ke Kapena. Ke hoopaa o ka hora

DATE. MANAWA.	NAMES. NA INOA.	STATIONS. OIHANA.	ADVANCE. KUU I LOOA E.		WAGES. KA UKU.		WITNESS. NA HOIKE.	AMOU UKU
			DOLLARS.	CENTS.	DOLLARS.	CENTS.		DOLLAR
October 21	Sapahula	Bout-Steerer	$45	"	1/75	Sig	C.S. Barton	
" "	Rumukahi	Sailor	30	"	1/130	"	"	
" "	Maka	"	30	"	1/130	"	"	
" "	Makai	"	35	"	1/130	"	"	
" "	Soro	"	35	"	1/130	"	"	
" "	Sonokeva	"	80	"	1/150	~	~	
" "	Mokai	"	30	"	1/150	"	"	
" "	Kanana	"	30	"	1/130	"	"	
" "	Enoka	"	30	"	1/130	"	"	
" "	Kahike	"	30	"	1/130			
" "	Kahui	"	30	"	1/130			
" "	Kalohilaw	"	30	"	1/125		~	
" 22	Keleia	"	30	"	1/115			
" "	Waihia	"	35		1/115			

LES.

...nau inoa malalo, ke ae aku nei makou, a ke hoopaa nei makou ia
...ope o ko makou mau inoa, maluna o ka   i kapaia
...o   .   ke Kapena, i keia manawa,
   e holo ana no i '

   a e hoi mai paha o ua   i keia
...i mamua o ka pau ana o ua mau malama   la-
...e hana no i ka makou oihana a pau me ka oiaio, ima paha maluna
...a ma na waapa, i ka po paha i ke ao paha e like me na luina mai-
...na o ua moku la i kapaia o   a pau ia
...keia mea o makou i ka uku a pau e like me ke kakau ana mahope
..."Ka Uku." No ka oiaio o keia hoolimalima, ua kakau mua ia
...ou ia makou iho a ee maluna o ia moku i ka
   i ka la   o   18 .

SECURITY. MEA HOOPAA PU.	REMARKS. OLELO HOOLAHA.
P. Mahaolema	All Native Seamen are to be paid and discharged before the officer appointed under the Act of June 25/56 The Ship Master will pay to the Shipping Officer 50c on Shipping & 50c on discharging each Seamen —

The Kanaka Connection

*T*heir names were Lono, Kalohilau, Makai, Keleia, and they and thousands like them would provide a heaven-sent answer to a serious manpower problem of the whaleships in the Pacific. Whaling was a labor intensive industry, and as crew members deserted, or died, or were dumped ashore, whaleships needed replacements quickly.

The Hawaiians proved to be the perfect choice — so much so that the monarchy demanded a bond of $200 be deposited for each 'kanaka' hired, to be forfeited if the sailor was not returned home within one year. *Kanaka,* incidentally, is the Hawaiian word for 'man' and was used loosely by the whalers to identify all Pacific native islanders.

These Hawaiian Shipping Articles, dated October 21, 1856 at Lahaina, Maui are printed in Hawaiian and English and stipulate that:

We, whose names are hereunto affixed, do hereby agree and bind ourselves to serve in the capacities set opposite our respective names, on board the Bark called the Tamerlane...*now lying at the port of Lahaina and bound on a whaling cruise...And we further agree, that during said voyage we will perform our duty faithfully, whether on board said ship* Tamerlane *or in her boats, whether by night or day, as good obedient seamen."*

The *Tamerlane* was signing on fourteen Kanakas, one as a 'boatsteerer' (or harpooneer) and the others as sailors. Literally *half* her crew was being replaced in Lahaina by Hawaiians for the winter cruise near the Equator. This document is mute testimony not only to the desirability of Hawaiians as whalers, but to the inherent problems the captains had in keeping a crew together once they reached Hawai'i.

And in 1868, Welshman Theo H. Davis founded the firm which still bears his name. All four of these companies once profited handsomely from provisioning the vast whaling enterprise.

Aside from hardware — harpoons, rope, barrels, sails, — the whalers needed foodstuffs and crewmen. Small farms provided fresh fruits and vegetables, and ranches provided beef and pork. The ranches of Kohala and Waimea on the Big Island —including Parker Ranch — and the hillside farms of Kula on the slopes of Maui's Haleakala, were started primarily to provision ships and are still going strong today.

The whaleships' other great need in Hawai'i was for crewmen to replace those who had jumped ship or been lost enroute. Hawaiians were the perfect choice. E. S. Allen writes in *Children of the Light* , "One factor that continued to attract the Yankee whaler to the Islands was the availability of manpower. The Hawaiian was a sailor by instinct, a superb boatman, and the average whaling master was eager to sign him on not only because of this, but because he was also likeable and industrious."

By the 1840s, perhaps a third of the crew members on most Pacific whalers were Hawaiians, and by the 1860s, the percentage was half. This migration of young men to the whaleships — often never to return home to the Islands — had a profound impact on the fabric of Hawaiian society.

Other Hawaiians were moving to larger towns to work or sell their wares, causing many rural villages to disappear. More and more foreigners — missionaries, businessmen, seamen, bums — were making Hawai'i home. These factors, coupled with a catastrophic mortality in the native Hawaiian population due to Western diseases to which they had no hereditary resistance, were changing the face of Hawai'i, both rapidly and forever.

Captain Cook had estimated the native Hawaiian population at some 400,000 in 1789, and current researchers believe that the number may actually have been as high as 800,000. By the census of 1872 — eighty-three years later — the number had fallen to less than 50,000. "Civilization" and "Progress" had taken an awful toll.

Meanwhile the two whaling ports, Lahaina and Honolulu, were increasing in both population and importance. The trans-shipment of oil and whalebone — so that the whalers could unload and go back out to fill their holds again — was becoming commonplace, and merchant ships, especially clippers, were visiting Hawai'i more frequently. As whaling began to decline after 1852, the trans-shipping trend became even more pronounced, and in that next decade alone, some eighteen million gallons of

Above: King Kameameha III was monarch for almost thirty years, from 1825 until 1854. During his reign, the whaling industry became the economic mainstay of the Islands, and Kamehameha was finally able to satisfy the national debt accumulated years earlier. His was a reign fraught with pressures on both the monarchy itself and on the Hawaiian people. France, England and the United States all vied for influence, occasionally with gunboats, and Hawaiians continued to die in astonishing numbers — their bodies contaminated by Western diseases and their spirits broken, according to historian John Dominis Holt, by the missionaries' "thunderous denunciations of their traditional beliefs." Kamehameha himself died a young man of forty.

whale oil, and fourteen million pounds of whalebone, passed through Hawaiian ports.

And thousands upon thousands of whaling men continued to pass through Hawaiian ports as well. As the numbers increased — in 1846 there were 596 visits by whaleships, each with some thirty crewmen — the problems increased too, and in November 1852 they culminated in the infamous Whalers' Riot.

Honolulu Harbor had almost 150 ships moored, just returned from a successful season on the Japan Grounds. That number represented close to two thousand celebrating sailors on shore, many of whom ended up in police custody for various offenses. One Henry Burns, off the *Emerald*, was not quite ready to quiet down even after he had been incarcerated in the old fort. He began tearing up the floor of his cell and throwing the bricks at his jailers. A wooden nightstick silenced Henry. Permanently. As word of his demise spread through the well-lubricated crowd of whalers, a cry went up for the guard responsible, and the police station was set ablaze. Several stores burned to the ground, and only a lucky shift in the wind prevented the whaleships in the harbor — their holds bulging with casks of oil — from catching fire. The whalers rampaged through the night and on into the next-day and were finally defused by a combination of angry citizens and throbbing hangovers. It was a near miss both for the city and the fleet.

Hawai'i businessmen were quick to capitalize on the opportunity to provision whalers but slow to actually get into the whaling business themselves. It was not until the mid-1850s — in hindsight way too late — that a local whaling industry really took hold. By 1854, there were six Hawai'i-registered vessels, and four years later there were nineteen.

With some six-sevenths of the world's whaling fleet scouring the Pacific for the Leviathan, hunting became harder. It was always an inexact science, and whaler Charles Nordhoff (grandfather of the *Mutiny on the Bounty* author) wrote, "The discovery of a school may be properly counted under the head of the chapter on accidents." There has always been some question as to whether the whale population was decimated by the whalemen, or if the whales simply became warier and moved on. In the case of the sperm whale, evidence is mounting to support the latter theory — they went elsewhere.

As the herds of sperm whales became more difficult to find around Japan, ships ventured further north to the Bering Sea. In 1848, the bark *Superior*, under Captain Roys, ventured through the narrow Bering Strait between Alaska and Siberia and spent the summer whaling in the Arctic Sea. She returned with a hold full of oil and bone, and once again, the fleet

followed the lead to new grounds. There they found both different whales and different conditions. Instead of the sperm whale, which rarely ventured out of temperate waters, they hunted the bowhead — a filter-feeder cousin of the right whale — with a mouth full of flexible strips of baleen.

By the early 1850s, many outside events would have a tremendous impact on the business of whaling for profit. In 1849, there had been a California Gold Rush of immense proportions, and the whalers had sold travel accomodations to as many passengers as they could jam into their already overcrowded

Above: An elderly Hawaiian gentleman rests on his sea chest — a remnant of a youth spent on a whaleship, perhaps? This rare photograph from Bishop Museum's Archives, was taken about the turn of the century.

ships. Likely as not, by the time these ships reached San Francisco, the crew had gold fever as badly as the passengers, and they'd all leave for the gold fields together. San Francisco Bay was littered with over 500 abandoned ships — whaling and otherwise — with no one to sail them anywhere. For a time they served as floating warehouses and rented rooms, but eventually most of them just sank at their moorings.

A Whaling Family

*T*he proud Yankee visages peering forth above are those of New Bedford whaling master Abraham Wilcox Peirce, his wife Harriet, and their daughter Hattie —pictured with both her mother and father in daguerrotype images taken several years apart.

Captain Peirce first visited these Islands in 1840. He realized early that whaling was a dying industry and invested his profits in Hawai'i property, both in commercial lands out near Pearl Harbor and a home downtown at the corner of School and Queen Emma.

Captain and Mrs. Peirce's younger daughter, Sarah, (not pictured here) led a fascinating life. She graduated from Punahou and then entered Boston Medical School — the first woman to do so. A furor erupted among male students, and she was expelled after two weeks. Later re-admitted, she graduated with an M.D. near the top of her class. In 1885, Sarah Peirce married Dr. N.B. Emerson in Honolulu, and they devoted their entire lives to preserving the chants, hulas and traditions of ancient Hawai'i.

The First Whaleship Photo

New Bedford Whaling Museum

*T*his rare, never-before-published picture is the first documented photograph ever taken of a whaleship. This ambrotype, on silver-coated glass, was taken of the storm-battered *Benjamin Tucker* in Honolulu Harbor during December 1856, probably by photographer Hugo Stangenwald. The ambrotype above was commissioned by Captain Albert Barber to give the whaleship's New Bedford owners an idea of the damage that she had suffered enroute to Hawai'i.

According to her logbook, the *Benjamin Tucker* was "Bound for the Sandwich Islands" from a whaling voyage in the Arctic. She was some 1700 miles due north of Honolulu when a storm struck. The ship's log of Monday, November 3, 1856, tells the story: "This 24 hours is very unlucky for us. Heavy gale from NW and a very heavy sea. At 9pm mainmast went by the board about 15' from the deck and that took the mizzen topmast with it. Stove the bulwarks on the starboard side. Stove 3 boats. All hands employed in clearing away the spars and rigging. Making water fast and broke the tiller." By Thursday the 6th of November, they were underway again, as they had "got up a jerrymast and set main topsail." Six long leaky weeks after the storm, the *Benjamin Tucker* finally limped into Honolulu on December 16, after averaging less than two knots with their two "jerryrigged" masts.

The following letter accompanied the photograph:

> Capt. Thos. Spencer of Honolulu
> presents his compliments to Messer.
> Chas. R. Tucker & Co. of New Bedford
> and begs their acceptance of the
> accompanying daguerreotype which will
> give them some idea of the appearance
> of the ship *Benjamin Tucker* on her
> arrival at this port.
> Honolulu, 1st January 1857

Captain Thomas Spencer — who wrote the letter above — was both a ship chandler who would profit from the *Tucker's* repairs and a legendary character in the Hawai'i of the mid-1800s. He had been master of the New Bedford whaleship *Triton*, and was one of the lucky survivors when she was attacked by natives of Nonouti Island, along the Equator, in January 1848. Two months later, he arrived in Honolulu and abandoned the sea forever. He became a successful ship chandler and confidant of Hawaiian royalty. Spencer took credit for blocking a proposed 1853 annexation of the Islands to the United States and also founded Honolulu's first hook-and-ladder company. When whaling fortunes started to decline, he moved to Hilo, where he continued to provision ships, and started a sugar plantation called *Amaulu.*

Meanwhile, the rest of the fleet was steered well clear of the temptations of California gold by their captains. The bowheads in the Bering Sea were numerous, but so was the competition to catch them, and the whaling season that far north was much shorter. Risks of failure were also far greater, and many New England ship owners were winding down their operations — unwilling or unable to take the chances required to continue whaling.

To make matters worse, in 1859 a hole drilled down 69' into bedrock in Titusville, Pennsylvania, gushed petroleum, and soon the area was booming. This oil from the ground, cheaper and certainly easier to get, would soon begin to replace whale oil in lamps and for machinery lubrication.

As if the migration of the fleet into the more dangerous Arctic waters and the discovery of petroleum weren't enough, on April 12, 1861, the Confederacy attacked Fort Sumter, South Carolina, and the War Between The States was on. And once again, a war would prove disastrous to the whaling fleet. Three heavily-armed Confederate gunboats — the *Sumter*, the *Alabama*, and the *Shenandoah* — would burn and sink forty-six whaleships from the South Atlantic to the North Pacific. Forty more would form the *Stone Fleet*, a group of old whalers bought by the Union and fitted in New Bedford for a very special task. Their whaling gear was pulled off and auctioned, and area farmers were asked to collect rocks and bring them to the harbor. Holes were drilled, then plugged, in the vessels' hulls, and the holds were filled with New England granite, dragged there on "stone sleds" pulled by teams of draft horses. The ships were sailed to the mouth of the harbor at Charleston, S.C. where their bungs were pulled out to scuttle them as a blockade. The weight of the stones plunged them deep into the muck of the harbor bottom, and they were totally ineffectual in stopping the Confederate raiders.

In Hawai'i, it was becoming painfully clear — even to the myopic — that the glory days of whaling were fading fast, and the search for an economic successor was in full swing. By 1862, David L. Gregg, the monarchy's Minister of Finance, wrote, "We are in a sort of transitional state, turning from nearly a total dependence on the whale fisheries of the northern seas to the internal resources of the country." Gregg was referring to sugar cane, a crop which would soon rescue the Hawaiian economy in the nick of time, just as whaling had earlier saved the day when the sandalwood trade faded.

The Civil War, whose warships almost destroyed the whaling business, helped to establish sugar as heir to the Islands' economic throne. In the United States, sugar was grown in the Deep South, which had seceded from the Union, so the market was wide open. Hawai'i's exports of sugar increased tenfold between the war years of 1860 and 1865.

As sugar's fortunes began to soar, the Islands' flexible businessmen responded by shifting capital into sugar plantations to survive, while continuing to supply the ever-dwindling number of whaleships searching for bowheads in the frozen North.

Below: A lithograph of the Stone Fleet *about to embark from New Bedford in an attempt to block Confederate harbors.*

Lahaina Whaling Museum

但軍艦之由
船長四十六間余

幅二拾二間余
右

傳馬船八艘
但長五間半幅二間余

人数八百人
但大将マリキ子タ四人職上下ク自之由
小筒八百挺 副将コロ子ル

大筒六十四挺
但二挺傳九右三十二挺宽 桅筒五百挺

帆柱長四十八間余

前柱長三十六間余
亮三賣目位ノ筒

後柱長三十九間余

外委細ニ不知

An Historic Rescue Mission

一時弘化二巳年三月十日浦賀湊入津
亜米利加之船圖

*T*he whalers had hunted in the Sea of Japan since 1820, but had never made landfall because Japan's borders had been sealed to foreigners for some two centuries. Sailors unlucky enough to be shipwrecked there were mistreated or killed. Credit for opening Japan to the outside world has always gone to U.S. Navy Commodore Matthew C. Perry, who led a task force of warships into Urago (now Tokyo) Bay in 1853. With an elaborate show of both ceremony and force, Perry compelled the reluctant emperor to sign a trade treaty with the United States.

But Commodore Perry wasn't the first American to successfully negotiate with Japan. In March 1845 — fully eight years before Perry — the Yankee whaler *Manhattan* under Captain Mercator Cooper sailed into Urago Bay with twenty-one Japanese fishermen whom they had rescued in the North Pacific.

Cooper wanted to return the shipwrecked sailors to their homeland, but the suspicious Japanese officials refused. Cooper persisted. After three weeks, Japan relented and allowed the *Manhattan* to drop anchor and land her passengers. They also ordered her surrounded and guarded by hundreds of boats filled with armed samurai.

The Japanese were fascinated by the "big junk" and came aboard her with a group of artists to document the ship, the equipment and the crew. This watercolor on rice paper shows a pair of unusual American flags and a black crewman as lookout.

The Kanji characters describe length and width of the *Manhattan* and the height of her three masts in *ken* — a measurement of about six feet. Characters also record the date and other details: "Koka second year (1845) March 12 — Uraga Harbor Arrival of American Ship — 8 small boats, large cannon, small cannons."

Danger in the Arctic

Follow, follow the whales to the very top of the Earth, follow until daylight never ends, until your world is reduced to just three colors — a glaring white, the icy green of the ocean and, when you're lucky, the bloody red decks of your ship. Risk everything you've ever had to follow the Leviathan into this Hell froze over.

As the 1860s wound to a close, the industry was in its death throes. Fewer whaleships sallied forth to chase fewer whales. As petroleum filled more and more lamps, the market for whale oil continued to shrivel, and the whalers concentrated on the baleen "whalebone" used as raw material to manufacture buggy whips, umbrella ribs and corset stays.

Long lengths of whalebone were a product which the bowhead whale in the Arctic had in abundance. Occasionally, if the oil market was particularly down, the whalers didn't bother to 'try out' their oil-rich blubber (up to 28" thick), but would just kill the whales, yank out the baleen, and abandon the rest.

By this time, the whaleships were venturing hundreds of miles above the Arctic Circle into frigid Polar seas. The whaling season in these waters was extremely short, and ice floes were a constant threat. The ships had been double-hulled as an added measure of safety, though once caught in the pack ice, they were goners, double-hulled or not. These were tricky seas to sail — magnetic compasses would give false readings so close to the Pole — and the pack ice would shift quickly, cutting off escape. The weather was often foggy, which made navigation even more difficult. Each year, it seemed, a ship or two would be lost to the elements or barely manage to escape when it strayed too far or stayed too long.

Success in the Arctic was often less a matter of skill than of luck, which is a tough way to run a business. The price for miscalculation was high, but whalers

Left: *An original oil painting dating to the late 1860s, titled "Bowheading in the Arctic Ice."*

knew the risks, and the later they stayed in the fall, the greater those risks were. In the season of 1870, the New Bedford bark *Japan* was crushed in the ice near East Cape with a loss of nine men. Captain Frederick Barker and twenty-four survivors spent the winter with Eskimos and were rescued the next summer by returning whalers. During the interminable Arctic winter, Barker and his men learned first-hand the plight that their reckless hunting was causing the natives. They were killing the bowheads, which Eskimos sometimes hunted for food, but far worse was that, armed with surplus Civil War rifles, whalers had taken to slaughtering walruses — at least *150,000* of them in one five-year period — on which the Eskimos depended for their survival.

Captain Barker and his men saw for themselves just how desperate the situation was for these people living on the very edge, but despite his protestations and others, the killing of walruses went on unabated.

The next season, 1871, a disaster of monumental proportions befell the Arctic fleet. The Eskimos had predicted it, but their warnings went unheeded as superstitious mutterings by the whalers. In August, an early — very early — cold front swept down off the Polar ice cap. A biting North Wind swirled across seas already thickening to slush and encrusted the whaleships in ice. The masters of the Arctic Fleet soon realized that escape was well nigh impossible.

They were trapped in the ferocious grip of Arctic winter. Thirty-two whaleships — pride of the fleets of New England, Honolulu and San Francisco — would slowly, surely, be compressed to splinters by the ice.

Thirty-two ships, and their valuable cargos of oil and whalebone, doomed to a common Arctic grave. They had one last hope — to strip the light Honolulu bark *Kohala* of all possible weight and float her out over a shoal. That, too, failed, and the masters knew then that their ships, their pride, and their way of life were beyond saving. Now only with the utmost luck would the 1220 souls aboard their ships be saved.

Another Honolulu bark, the *Comet*, was the first to be shattered by the expanding ice. "Every timber broken," Captain Silva noted on September 2, and his crew was divided up among the other ships. And still the weather worsened as the remaining whaleships lay storm-anchored in the only liquid left — a narrow channel of water with rocky Alaska beach on one side and creeping pack ice on the other.

On September 9, the bark *Roman* met her end, as recounted by an astonishingly articulate crewman in

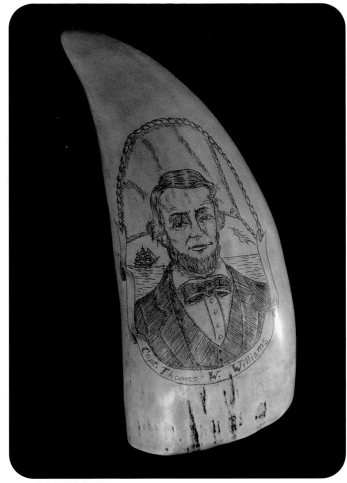

Snows were deepening and icy seas continued to clamp ships in place — just prior to crushing them.

By the morning of September 14, hundreds of whaleboats were loaded with people carrying a few cherished possessions, ready to begin the dangerous eighty-mile trek towards the seven rescue vessels nervously awaiting them to the south. 1,219 souls, at least half of them Hawaiians, sailed miles through the rough seas, and dragged their heavily-laden whaleboats over the solid stretches of ice.

It was a fantastically perilous journey under terrible conditions, yet the entire group — 1211 men, three masters' wives and five children — all reached the refuge of the seven ships off Icy Cape. There they were literally crammed aboard for the long trip from the icy Arctic wastes to tropical Honolulu, where they arrived by early November.

Only one man, by his own choice, stayed behind with the trapped fleet in hopes of being able to claim what he could the next Spring. He was the

an interview with Honolulu's *Pacific Commercial Advertiser*, "The floe caught the ship on each side, and lifted her up bodily, keel out. Relaxing its grip for an instant, the ship settled between the icy jaws of the floe, when, coming together again, she was crushed like an eggshell, into atoms, and as the spasmodic relaxation again occured, she disappeared, leaving not a vestige of the lately noble vessel in sight, forty-five minutes from the time the ice first closed upon her."

Two days later, another ship, the *Awashonks*, imploded in the ice, and the masters of the trapped fleet decided to launch an expedition in whaleboats to search for seven ships further south which they desperately hoped had not left already or also been trapped in the ice. At that very moment, those seven ships actually *were* trapped, but finally parted their anchor chains and broke free.

When the boats reached them with word of the fleet's dire predicament, they immediately decided to abandon whaling and help with the rescue. James Dowden, master of the *Progress*, summed it up for the rest: "Tell them I will wait for them as long as I have an anchor left or a spar to carry a sail."

Even as the expedition took this message to the trapped fleet, the situation there was growing worse.

Facing page: Whaleboats from the trapped fleet brave the icy seas one last time, as they head for the seven rescue ships.
Above left: This scrimshawed tooth depicts an unlucky man, who lost not one, but two, ships in the Arctic ice. In 1871 he was master of the Monticello, crushed in the disaster at Belcher's Bay. In 1876 he was in command of the Clara Bell, *whose logbook (from an earlier voyage) is shown on pages 74-77, when it was lost in another early freeze in 1876.*
Above: A whaleship's rudimentary medicine chest, like the ones which proved fatal to the Eskimos.

sole witness to the Eskimos stripping what they could use from the abandoned whaleships. The masters had anticipated this looting and so had destroyed all the intoxicants aboard. But the Eskimos broke into the ship's medicine chests and devoured the contents, most of which made them deathly ill, and some of which made them dead. In a rage of fear and fury, they torched any ship to the waterline on which an Eskimo had become sick. The white man survived the long winter, without any booty, and later said, "A hundred and fifty thousand dollars would not tempt me to try another winter in the Arctic."

A few whalers tried a few more summers in the Arctic, but by then the message was clear: whaling was dead, or at least dying. Markets for oil and bone were drying up, and the impact on Hawai'i was enormous. The October 28, 1871 *Advertiser* noted:

"The absorbing topic of conversation in almost all circles throughout the community during the past week, has been the news, received on Monday, of the destruction of the North Pacific Whaling Fleet. And well may Honolulu pause and consider what will be the probable results to her own prospects from this sudden and unlooked for blow. There is not a single branch of industry in the Islands, not a man, woman or child, that will not, either immediately or remotely, feel the effects in the decreased circulation of money...To some branches of business in this city, the results will be disastrous in the extreme...Let no one flatter himself that he will not suffer with his neighbor. We are like a house built of cards — remove one, and the others tumble."

The days of hundreds of whaleships cramming Lahaina Roadsteads and Honolulu Harbor had long been over. But the economy of the nation of Hawai'i was still dependent, to some extent, on provisioning the whaling fleet. The Arctic ice that autumn of 1871 was the kiss of death. It was over now, just a fading memory, this whaling adventure of fifty-odd years.

Left: *Sheathed in copper stripped off the hull of their doomed ship, a whaleboat is dragged miles across jagged pack ice in this just-discovered 1873 painting by survivor James Gurrick.*

Hunted

To watch the humpbacks frolic in Maui's Ma'alea Bay, to see the newborn calves nuzzle their mothers, to hear the haunting refrains of the lovelorn giants, is a privilege. And it is ours only because a few brave individuals placed themselves between the harpoon cannons and the whales and said, "No more."

*W*hen the whaling industry was crushed — quite literally — in the Arctic pack ice of the 1870s, the great whales got a brief respite from their centuries-old role as targets. But then came a far more dangerous onslaught, this time from mechanized whalemen. To this new breed of predator, global extinction of the whale was immaterial, and they hunted with wanton abandon, going into the breeding grounds and killing mothers and calves at will.

Literally millions of these beautiful creatures were executed with exploding harpoons, then winched up a factory ship's ramp and turned into raw materials for such *vital* products as shoe polish, dog food, margarine, and tennis racket strings.

The beginnings of 'modern' whaling can be traced to a Norwegian sealer, Captain Svend Foyn. In 1864 he designed a steam whaleship, ironically, for the whales at least, called *Spes et Fides* (Hope and Faith). A cannon of his own invention was mounted on the prow. This deadly gun fired a harpoon with long barbs, which opened inside the whale like the ribs of a parasol. As these barbs unfolded, they broke a glass vial of sulphuric acid, triggering an explosion to kill the whale, an excruciating death that might last as long as two hours.

Left: "NYET" banner streaming, a Greenpeace Zodiac follows a Russian factory ship in the Arctic. The huge ramp in the stern is the slipway, on which whale carcasses are hauled for on-deck processing.

Foyn had, for all practical purposes, invented the whaling techniques and equipment that would be used to hunt the great whales to the brink of extinction in the 20th century. His invention was accepted, but not universally: American shipyards were still building wooden whalers as late as 1910.

Both early whalers and later ones went to sea to kill whales, but there were four important differences. The first was that modern technology eliminated all risk to the whaler himself, while his counterpart of a century ago was in constant danger from both the elements and the whale. Second was the use of bigger, faster ships capable of chasing and killing the fast rorqual whales — the immense blue, the fin, the sei — all of which could out-distance earlier whaleships. Third was the time factor: Yankee whalers might work round the clock for more than two days to process a big sperm, while modern whalers completed the job in less than an hour. And the fourth difference was that the new technologies for locating whales — underwater sonar, spotter planes and helicopters — were a far cry from a lookout clutching the mainmast scouting the horizon for vapor spouts.

By the 1870s, as recently discovered petroleum replaced whale oil, the 19th century whaling industry was near collapse, and the New England whaleship owners were shifting their investments to the sweatshops and textile mills closer to home. These were slightly less exploitive of labor than whaling had been, but the line was a fine one.

At the same time that the market for whale oil was decreasing, the fashion industry decreed that women looked especially fetching in enormous hoop skirts,

Rex Weyler/Courtesy Greenpeace Foundation Hawai'i

Above: This modern harpoon gun on the prow of a catcher-boat — its explosive tip set to detonate on contact — is far removed from a 19th century harpooneer braced in the front of a pitching whaleboat.

whose hoops of course had to be made from baleen. Off the whalers went again, back to the Arctic to hunt the bowhead, whose baleen plates could reach lengths of 14 feet. This was a particularly brutal trade. The whale was killed, his baleen torn out, and the carcass tossed overboard, blubber and all.

Soon iron-hulled steam whalers began to chug into polar seas, with explosive harpoon guns poking over their prows like figureheads of death. These ships — banked with snow as an insulating windbreak — could "winter over" in the occasional harbor, going back out to hunt as soon as warm spring winds began to break up the pack ice.

The Antarctic was next, and Foyn's inventions — steam whaler, explosive harpoon, and a hollow tube which inflated a sinking whale with compressed air — were keys to whaling in those southern waters. Rorquals — the huge blue and especially the extremely fast fin — were suddenly prime targets of these new technologies. In 1921 — a half-century after the Arctic ice destroyed the 19th century fleet — almost 12,000 whales were killed, and all but 751 sperms were from species which weren't even hunted by the earlier whalers.

Just ten years later, the whalers' total would almost quadruple, to over 41,000 animals, less than a hundred of them sperms. Technology made another giant leap in 1925 with the arrival in Antarctic waters of the *Lancing*, the first factory ship with a stern slipway to crank dead whales up a ramp for butchering. Survival for the whales looked even more grim when the Japanese fleets arrived in 1934, and the Russians followed in 1946.

Death tolls fluctuated year by year. As particular species were bludgeoned almost to extinction, their numbers diminished and other, less desirable species took their place as targets. Whaling had become a process of eradication, generated by nothing more than man's greed for dollars, or pounds, or rubles, or yen, and it reached its height in 1961 when 65,658 individual whales were destroyed — to make car wax, cat food, and lipstick.

By the early 60s it was clear that the severely depleted whale populations might never recover from slaughter on such a grand scale. A number of species had already been whaled into "commercial extinction," a frighteningly presumptuous term used by the industry to mean that they were no longer profitable to hunt. At that point they were placed on a protected list, so that stocks could regenerate and be hunted again. By 1966, five of ten marketable whales were already on that list: the right, bowhead, gray, blue and humpback — leaving the fin, sperm, sei, Minke's and Bryde's whales unprotected.

"Save the Whales!"

Courtesy Greenpeace Hawai'i Foundation

Top: *Earthtrust activists leaving Honolulu aboard* Sea Dragon *to confront the driftnet fleet in 1988.*
Left: *Greenpeace vs. the Russian whalers, 1976.*

Courtesy Earthtrust

*T*he Eisenhower Years in the 1950s were a very conservative, button-down era, but beneath the surface a revolution was brewing. In the 60s and 70s those feelings surfaced as radicalism, a time when the "status quo" mentality was challenged by people who not only wanted to rock the boat, but were willing to sink it. Right or wrong, people challenged, defied, then boldly changed "the system."

A black lady in Alabama refused to sit in the back of a bus, and the Civil Rights movement was born. An eighteen year old lit his draft card and ignited an anti-war crusade that finally toppled Lyndon Johnson's presidency and ended the war in Viet Nam. Constrained too long, a woman burned her bra and kindled the Women's Liberation movement.

The environment which we all shared got a new buzzword — Ecology — the interaction of natural forces. People objected to pollutants — oftimes toxic pollutants — in the air, the land and the water. Perhaps the crowning blow was the spontaneous combustion of Cleveland's Cuyahoga River.

People began to talk about Spaceship Earth and the inter-relationship of everyone and everything aboard it. "Save the Whales" became a rallying cry, and people who had never seen a whale — maybe never even seen an ocean — contributed dimes and dollars in an effort to save them. The direct-action environmental movement that resulted has since spawned campaigns which are today confronting the driftnetters, the loss of the tropical rainforests, offshore oil drilling, and more.

Excerpt (in blue) from a full page advertisement in The London Times on June 25, 1973.

One is killed every 20 minutes.
Is this carnage really necessary?

An open letter to the International Whaling Commission meeting in London today.

A 10-YEAR MORATORIUM ON COMMERCIAL WHALING should be passed at the IWC meeting:

1. To allow severely depleted whale populations to regenerate. Five species (blue, humpback, bowhead, right and gray) are now so reduced commercial exploitation is not profitable. As a result these species have been given total protection. The Fin Whale is at a low ebb, but still being exploited.

2. Whales are not indispensable to the human diet, nor are they essential to industry. Present uses for whale products — petfood, margarine, cosmetics, transmission oil — all have acceptable substitutes.

3. Whales exist in international waters; no one country (or even two) should assume, as they have done, the right to over-exploit them. Short-sighted exploitation has endangered long term prospects of the industry — not to mention the whales.

4. Catch controls have consistently been based on the most optimistic figures of populations when the only responsible procedure would be to err on the side of caution.

5. Relatively little is known about the social habits of whales or their ability to communicate seemingly, complex messages. Studies indicate that some cetaceans may possess a highly developed intelligence. It would be scientifically prudent and ethically sound to learn much more about whales before permitting any further reduction of the populations. Scientific study of living whales may well prove more about population structures and migrations than has been possible from the industrial catches. A moratorium could greatly stimulate such research. It will still be important to monitor whale populations as indicators of the well-being of the oceans and their ecosystems. We believe this can be done without killing them.

6. The method of killing can only be described as barbaric. The barbed, 160 lb. harpoon explodes inside the whale. Dying often takes up to half an hour and can take up to two hours.

7. We do not believe man any longer needs to hunt whales. The killing should stop, in the name of human dignity, at least until whale products are shown to be essential to human survival and a humane capture technique has been devised.

We the undersigned, belonging to many international conservation, natural history and scientific bodies urge all the delegates to the IWC to vote for a 10 year moratorium on all commercial whaling:

HRH Prince Bernhard
HRH The Duke of Edinburgh
Professor D.J. Kuenen
Laurence I. Moss
William A. Nierenberg
Cleveland Amory
John Aspinall
Dr. Gerardo PhD
Commander Jacques Cousteau
Professor Jean Dorst
Professor René Dubos PhD
Dr. Paul Ehrlich
Sir Frank Fraser Darling FRSE
Dr. Thor Heyerdahl PhD
Sir Julian Huxley FRS

Professor Claude Levi-Strauss
Dr. Konrad Lorenz
Dr. Sicco Mansholt
Sir Peter Scott CBE
Dr. J.E. Smith CBE, ScD, FRS
Animal Defence Society Limited
The Conservation Society
The Fauna Preservation Society
Friends of the Earth International
International Society for Protection of Animals
Project Jonah
Royal Society for Prevention of Cruelty to Animals
The Sierra Club
Universities Federation for Animal Welfare
World Wildlife Fund

THE INTERNATIONAL WHALING COMMISSION

...whether Leviathan can endure so wide a chase, and so remorseless a havoc; whether he must not at last be exterminated from the waters, and the last whale, like the last man, smoke his last pipe and then himself evaporate in the final puff.

Herman Melville, *Moby Dick*

In 1946, the International Whaling Commission was chartered "to protect all species of whales from further overfishing." For years the I.W.C. reacted only to the economic interests of its member nations. In 1974 the Mexican delegate predicted that "this Commission will be known to history as a small body of men who failed to act responsibly in the terms of a very large commitment to the world, and who protected the interests of a few whalers and not the future of thousands of whales."

Times, however, were changing, and the I.W.C. had to change with them. The original members all had whaling fleets, but as one after another succumbed to public pressure and stopped whaling, their delegations filled with anti-whaling activists. By 1986 a moritorium went into effect. After forty years of presiding over the slaughter of cetaceans, the I.W.C. — now primarily a body of conservationists — acted on the whales' behalf.

In 1971, the Congress asked the Secretary of State to negotiate a ten-year moratorium on all whaling. In 1972, the Marine Mammal Protection Act was passed, banning the killing of marine mammals within U.S. territorial waters or by American citizens anywhere in the world, it eliminated importation of any marine mammal products into the U.S. Congress strengthened the Endangered Species Act in 1973, adding further protection for the whales.

And still Russia and Japan went whaling — seemingly impervious to political pressures from other governments, bad press internationally and boycotts of Japanese and Russian goods organized by environmental groups. If none of these had much effect, what could possibly stop them?

It took a few brave souls, willing to take to the high seas and risk their lives, to challenge the whaleships. And because these young idealists filmed their dramatic exploits, the evening news featured their story all across the nation.

In 1975, members of Greenpeace pooled every penny they had to rent an elderly halibut seiner, the *Phyllis Cormack*. They headed for the Arctic in search of the Russian whaling fleet, and finding it, gave chase in tiny inflated Zodiacs.

Encouraged by their success, they chartered a larger vessel in 1976, the former mine sweeper *James Bay*. Michael Bailey, who later co-founded Earthtrust, was aboard and noted, "I could see fear in the young harpooner's eyes as we manuvered the Zodiac in between his gun and the whales. I was not 20' in front of his gun, with its explosive-tipped harpoon in the barrel. Not 20' behind him, ship's officers in orange suits screamed orders at him in Russian. Our bulky 16mm cameras whirred as the harpooner tried desperately to kill a whale and warn us away at the same time. If we positioned ourselves correctly, he'd miss the whale by a few feet and us by the same amount. Our goal was not only to protect the whales — with our own lives if need be — but to let the rest of the world see what was happening in these remote seas. We'd put in at Hawai'i or San Francisco to drop off film to be processed and sent out."

The impact was enormous. No one had ever tried a direct-action confrontational environmental campaign before, and no one knew if it would work. It was, as Bailey puts it, "a low budget, high energy project by people who were absolutely committed to

Below: During refueling operations in very rough seas, it was common for the small catcherboats to tie whales to their sides to act as giant cushions to prevent damage from the much larger factory ships.

Below: The image on this Japanese billboard, a hundred years out of date, shows a man in a small boat challenging a huge whale. The true picture — of whales tracked on sonar and slaughtered by exploding harpoons — is far less romantic.

全日本海員組合
伝統ある捕鯨を守ろう

CONTINUE THE WHALING ON SCIENTIFIC FACTS!

全日本海員組合 ALL JAPAN SEAMEN'S UNION

活力ある組合!

end the killing of whales. We never knew if we were about to run out of money, but we knew for certain we would *never* run out of determination."

In 1977, two ships set sail to intercept the Russians. The Vancouver-based *James Bay* confronted the Vladivostoc fleet off the U.S. West Coast. The *Ohana Kai,* out of Honolulu, was a 176' converted U.S. Navy sub chaser, with ten Zodiacs aboard. Chartered by Don White of Earthtrust Hawai'i, and the Greenpeace Foundation of Hawai'i, *Ohana Kai* successfully encountered and boarded the Dalniyvostoc fleet. An ABC News helicopter hovered nearby.

Once again each confrontation drew wide media response. The effect was astonishing, even to the protestors themselves. As Bailey described it, "We began getting support from governments, strong political support, and the pressure on the whaling nations increased." World opinion on whaling was galvanized, and people in cities and towns everywhere took to the streets in mass demonstrations.

In 1986 the International Whaling Commission's moratorium on commercial whaling — sought so long by conservationists — took effect, soon after Russia announced they were quitting.

"It was a great victory for conservationists — the moratorium at least gave us a *chance* to save the whales," says Don White, "and yet the whales are worse off today than they have ever been. Some populations are perilously thin. Pirate whaling and sound and chemical pollution pose significant dangers to the whales' survival. More ultra-violet radiation from the Greenhouse Effect threatens *krill*, a basic food supply. And driftnets appear to be responsible for the disappearence of young humpbacks. Only the gray whale has made a strong comeback from near-extinction. Survival of the blue, the right, the bowhead, and the fin remain seriously in question."

In addition, there is *still* "legal whaling" to contend with. Each year a number of whales are killed for "scientific research," in which they are studied momentarily by Japanese and Icelander scientists before heading to the markets of Japan.

The Japanese market for whale meat is the *driving* force behind whaling — it is the *only* economic justification to kill whales. If Japan were to follow the example of many other countries and ban the use of marine mammal products in any form, whaling could really end forever.

Pirate Whalers

It was almost midnight on a summer night in 1985 in the remote Korean harbor of Chiangsangpo. The old whaleship throttled down and slid next to its pier, a large right whale lashed alongside. Creeping around the shadowy wharf, two Earthtrust volunteers, Honolulu housewives Olivia Young and Caroline Takahashi, photographed the grisly operation. Spotting the flash, the ship's captain jumped ashore and struggled with Caroline, trying to grab her camera, with its film of his illegal activities.

Olivia rushed to Caroline's aid and was pinned to a warehouse wall by three crewmen, who began kicking and punching her. Well versed in martial arts, Olivia, 51, dispatched her attackers and then chased the captain back aboard his whaleship. When police arrived, Olivia was standing guard *under* the captain, cowering atop his radio mast.

The whalers were arrested for assault, and the Korean authorities, suffering international embarrassment because of the incriminating photos, agreed to shut down the pirate whaling industry operating out of Korea. Illegal whaling is profitable, though, as surplus catcherboats can be had for some $40,000, and a whaler can almost make that by killing just one whale! Earthtrust, therefore, carefully monitors the situation with undercover operations throughout the Orient.

Above: Olivia Young and Caroline Takahashi pose in front of a Korean pirate whaler, during their mission.
Below: Korean pirate whalers starting to flense a right whale, probably the most endangered of all whale species.

Stripmining the Sea

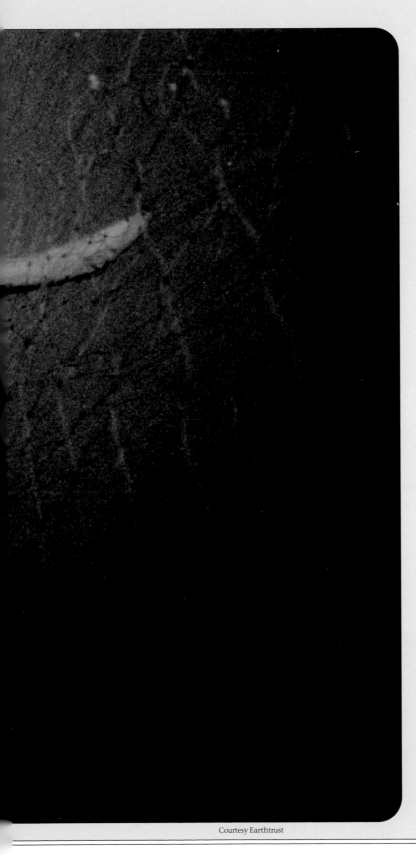

Courtesy Earthtrust

"It was like traversing a watery desert."
Sam LaBudde, Earthtrust 1988

*L*aBudde, a research biologist, is describing the central North Pacific — an area that has teemed with life for eons. The culprit is driftnetting, a technology threatening the ocean's ecological balance. Imagine a fine monofilament net 40' deep and 25 miles long that quite literally captures everything — dolphins, whales, turtles, even diving seabirds — in its path. Every night 1500 ships lay out almost 40,000 miles of driftnet, set at right angles to the prevailing currents. It is no wonder the seas there are a watery desert.

Driftnetting is outrageously wasteful, with often more than half the catch being thrown back *dead* into the ocean. It is also outrageously short-sighted, for it is so efficient that recent catches have been drastically smaller because there's less left to catch.

Most fisheries are species specific: aku longliners hook aku, lobstermen trap lobster, codders net cod. Driftnets, however are indescriminate mass murderers. The driftnetting fleet, from Japan, South Korea and Taiwan, follows the food chain — and hauls in everything that won't pass through a 3" square of knotted nylon. The effects have stunned Pacific fisheries — the 1988 salmon catch was projected at 44 million pounds and came in at barely 12!

Catalyzed by video images from the Earthtrust 1988 driftnet expedition, nation after nation — New Zealand, Australia, the United States, Vanuatu, the Cook Islands, Canada, and American Samoa — all banned driftnetting in their waters in 1989. Since 1981, Japan, driftnetting's largest practitioner, banned the practice *within a thousand miles* of its own coastal waters because it wrought havoc with its fisheries.

"Ghost nets" lost in the ocean, their nylon essentially indestructable, continue fishing on their own, sinking when the weight of the catch gets too great and rising to fish again when the animals have rotted.

Driftnetting literally threatens the ecosystem of the world's oceans. It must be stopped!

Right: *A dolphin, drowned in a North Pacific driftnet, which was invisible to its echo-location sonar.*

Dolphin Mind

"Diviner than the dolphin is nothing yet created; for indeed they were aforetime men and lived in cities along with mortals, but...exchanged the land for the sea and put on the form of fishes."

Ancient Greek poet Oppian

Dolphins have been a mystical presence to Man ever since the Ancient Greeks believed that they were gods who had originally been mortals. Man may be descended from simians, but in many ways we feel more affinity for dolphins. Extremely intelligent, playful and nurturing of their young, these animals have always struck a special chord.

Except for California grays and certain humpback herds that spend time in accessible areas, most great whales are almost impossible to study in nature. Their size, movements, and habitat make it just too difficult to access them and control the experiments. But dolphins are easy to study and, in fact, have been the subjects of numerous studies for years. Researchers of every specialty of science have been awed by the intelligence of dolphins. They are quick learners with prodigious memories, who seem to truly enjoy interacting with people.

Discounting such aquarium show tricks as dunking basketballs and "doing the hula" (tailwalking) to piped-in ukulele music, there is serious work going on to better understand the dolphins. Researchers are focusing on their language and echo-location (sonar) skills. Even more advanced research is concentrating on inter-species communication.

Can humans communicate with dolphins? On a certain level, we have always communicated with animals and vice-versa. Spanking a puppy for swiping a steak off the table is a form of inter-species communication. When we talk of inter-species communication with dolphins, however, we are referring to an entirely different dimension of thought transfer. People

Left: *Pacific spotted dolphin, Stenella attenuata.*

127

If you yourself can withstand three cheers at be-holding these vivacious fish, then heaven help ye; the spirit of godly gamesomeness is not in ye."

Herman Melville

doing research in this field dream of actually communicating back and forth with cetaceans, but realize that evolution may have made both species too wildly divergent for much conversation.

Don White, currently researching dolphin communication, says, "Whales have such large brains, and they're so different from us, that I don't think any meaningful abstract communication has occured between man and the large whales. As to whether it's even possible, I think that'll be for generations beyond our own. Dolphins, however have brains about the same size as ours, and our experiments seem to be demonstrating just how bright they actually are. Since sound is their primary mode of perception, we can speculate that sound may also be their primary mode of expression. It is possible that they communicate through a language of sonic pictures.

"We are able to hear the sounds dolphins make, but may be interpreting them differently, just as TV and FM radio both broadcast by frequency modulation, but one is transmiting pictures and the other words and music. If humans were FM radio stations and dolphins were TV transmitters, one or the other would need to adapt to make true inter-species communication possible.

"Our experimental research program, Project Delphis, grew out of a belief that dolphins will not survive as a species unless people learn to see them as truly intelligent beings, rather than as fish. The goal is to establish a baseline of dolphin intelligence, using an open-ended format, which imposes no expectation on their responses.

"We are creating a sonic keyboard to allow the dolphins to interact with a computer screen and a variety of computer programs, which the dolphins can select at will. The key is that the dolphins will be in control of everything — there will be no humans in the loop. From the dolphins' interaction with the computer programs, we will extrapolate the precise logical steps they took to arrive at specific responses. This should demonstrate, at the very least, a clear ability for rational, sequential thought."

A 1980 Marine Mammal Fund publication on the dolphin reports, "Though it is pointless to make comparisons between the intelligence of these small whales and that of man, stories abound of the actions and antics of dolphins which indicate that they are amazingly bright. For example, a heavy wind blows over the dolphin tanks at Marineworld/Africa USA in Redwood City, California, and head dolphin trainer, Jim Mullen, has taught several dolphins to retrieve pieces of trash blown into the tank. For each piece of trash returned, the animal receives a fish. One dolphin continuously retrieved more trash than the others. Incredibly, this dolphin had stored several bags and a rope under a platform. He then swam down, tore off a small piece, and returned to the surface for his reward. The notable phenomenon is that this dolphin devised his 'savings account' without any model or training. Mullen reports that since this incident, most of the dolphins in that tank have learned to keep stashes of their own."

According to Dr. Sterling Bunnel, "The cetacean system (compared to man's) appears to be a more integrated and contemplative one, evolved in conditions where immediate danger was not so likely as it was for most mammals. It is ironic that man's technology, developed as an adaptation to danger, now presents the whales with dangers for which their own evolutionary history leaves them quite unprepared."

Programs for Earthtrust's Project Delphis are currently being written using a Mac II and large color monitors. The project will invite the dolphins to demonstrate intelligence and inventiveness by interacting with the computer screen.

Photograph by Rick Peterson

The Flipper Seal of Approval

Almost without question the cruelest and most meaningless death for dolphins occurs during purse-seining for tuna. Only a miniscule percentage of tuna is actually caught in this way, but the technique results in the deaths of tens of thousands — more likely hundreds of thousands — of dolphins each year. The method began more than thirty years ago in 1957 and exploited the fact that schools of large yellowfin tuna swim beneath herds of dolphins. The dolphins are easy to spot and the purse-seiners would chase them with speedboats and explosives, then encircle the tiring dolphins with a huge net, some 600' deep and 3/4 of a mile long. The two ends of the net are connected and drawn together like a purse, trapping the dolphins — and if the fishermen are lucky — some tuna. Dolphins are drowned, or crushed in the net's winch as the catch is hoisted aboard. Only 5% of the world's tuna is caught this way, and this is the only method that destroys dolphins. So how can we tell if our tuna-fish sandwich, on toast with mayo and lettuce, was caught by purse-seining or not? The truth is we can't, but the Flipper Seal can... Licensed to the tuna industry, the Flipper Seal on a can of tuna will assure the buyer that purse-seining was not used, and that no dolphins died in the process. Earthtrust's Flipper Seal program begins January 1, 1990.

The Whale's Song

From space, the planet is blue.
From space, the planet is the territory
Not of humans, but of the whale.
Blue seas cover seven-tenths of the earth's surface,
And are the domain of the largest brain ever created,
With a fifty-million-year-old smile.

Heathcote Williams
Whale Nation

"***F***rom space, the planet is blue" and space is indeed the key word here, for it was only when we reached out for the moon and looked back at our home planet, that we saw more clearly our place in the universe, as a part of a larger mysterious whole.

What has triggered us to spend billions of dollars and thousands of man hours to hurl a few citizens into space? What need has driven us to build giant radio telescopes pointing into outer space to Search for Extra-Terrestrial Intelligence, or SETI?

Left: A humpback whale in Hawaiian waters, suspended in song.

Imagine for a moment meeting intelligent air-breathing creatures who live in the vast depths of space. Unaffected by gravity, they float in an atmosphere hundreds of times more dense than our own. Never in the dark, they carry their own three-dimensional sound illumination, and can literally see inside you, like an x-ray machine.

Imagine these foreign creatures, with so great an understanding of their own environment that they can use it to send and receive messages to each other over thousands of miles.

They have never discovered fire, nor created any tools or technology, yet they have established dominion in their world. Within that dominion they play and fight and love in an elaborate social structure, supporting each other when in need.

Imagine coming face to face with these creatures, perhaps a thousand times larger than you, and being met with an intense, but gentle curiosity. Imagine all of this, and you have encountered *the whale*.

According to Professor Teizo Ogawa of the University of Tokyo, "In the world of mammals there are two mountain peaks, one is Mount Homo Sapiens, and the other Mount Cetacean."

Isn't it strange then, that in our endeavors to find intelligence other than our own, mankind has chosen to look into outer space, rather than, in Jacques Cousteau's words, to the "inner space" of our oceans?

Right: *Close-up of a humpback whale.*

A closer look at "Mount Cetacean" reveals some amazing facts about whales. The blue whale, for example, is the largest animal ever to inhabit the earth, bigger even than the fossilized dinosaurs of old or the ephemeral Loch Ness Monster of today. Its heart is the size of a Volkswagen bug, and its arteries are large enough for a man to swim through. A sperm whale can dive to a depth of at least two miles — where the pressure on its body goes from 14 pounds per square inch to over 4000 — and can hold its breath for well over an hour. Humpbacks can build up enough blubber in four months in their feeding grounds that they need not eat for the other eight months of migration.

They catch their food by sending bubbles to the surface, which encircle the krill like a gigantic net.

Our search for understanding the nature of the Leviathan has led us to a fascination with the sounds of the whale, especially the songs of the humpback. Humpbacks have no vocal cords, and their stylized and intricate compositions are performed by shifting air back and forth between sacs in the head. Often longer than symphonic movements, the songs are performed in medleys that can last for as long as 22 hours. Although the music can change dramatically from year to year, each whale in an ocean-wide population sings the same song.

"The lesson is not about whales and dolphins, but about ourselves...Though the search for extra-terrestrial intelligence may take a very long time, we could not do better than to start with a program of rehumanization by making friends with the whales and dolphins."

Carl Sagan

After her 1987 trip to Maui, Boston Globe reporter Dianne Dumanoski wrote, "Sometimes when the engine is off and the boat is drifting on the turquoise waters off the old whaling port of Lahaina, the sound comes up right through the hull. If you happen to be swimming, you can feel vibrations, strong tingling vibrations. When researcher Deborah A. Glockner-Ferrari reaches for a hydrophone and drops it over the side of the boat, music — bizarre and beautiful — bursts forth.

"Long low rumbles; high, rising squeaks like a door opening slowly on rusty hinges; shrill whistles; grunts; moans; bursts of staccato 'brrrrrrs'; an eerie cello-like groaning. It sounds like half a dozen performers joined in a wild underwater symphony, but the whole repertoire is coming from a single animal.

"Directly below, perhaps sixty feet down, a humpback whale is hanging motionless in the crystalline deep and making whale music. And with his squeaks, moans, and meandering pure notes, the invisible soloist — making all these sounds without releasing air and without vocal chords — isn't just singing a humpback song, he's singing the particular song in fashion this year."

Left: A breaching Humpback frolics off the coast of Maui, like a 40-ton tourist.

Above: Humpback whale flukes have unique pigmentation which allows researchers to permanently identify individual animals. Careful records of their sightings are kept in order to determine life cycles and migration patterns.

Many people have been deeply moved by these extraordinary sounds, and have dedicated their lives to understanding them. Researchers Deborah and Mark Ferrari spend six months each year studying humpbacks during their annual visits to the Hawaiian Islands. Dr. Louis Herman of the University of Hawai'i Kewalo Basin Marine Research Facility, recorded and edited the sounds which were played to lure Humphrey the Wayward Whale back to the sea from his detour up the Sacramento River.

Each researcher has their own theory about the whales' songs. Graduate student Kevin Chu noted that the length of each whale's song varies considerably, and suggested a female may choose as a mate the male with the longest song. Jim Darling, of the West Coast Whale Research Foundation in Vancouver, believes the songs are part of a dominance ritual.

The best-known studies began in 1967 when Roger and Katharine Payne recorded the vocalizations of humpbacks from a small sailboat off Bermuda. Repeating the process each spring for five years, their recordings suggested that humpback solos were not random sounds, but were composed of regular repeating patterns. In 1971, the Paynes released an LP recording called "Songs of the Humpback Whale" which sold 125,000 copies and inspired songs by Judy Collins and Pete Seeger, as well as a concerto premiered by the N.Y. Philharmonic Orchestra.

NASA sent the song of the humpback into space in the unmanned Voyager probe along with human voices, as a representation of the diversity of life on earth. The recent movie *Star Trek IV* was based on the song of the humpback, and actor/director Leonard Nimoy later joined with jazz artist Paul Winter to record a haunting album called "Whales Alive," blending whale songs with contemporary music.

Most recently, biologists Katharine Payne of Cornell University and Linda Guinee from Long Term Research Institute in Massachusetts, proposed the theory that whales, like humans, use rhyme as an aid to memorize complex songs. In analyzing 548 whale songs with a sound spectrograph, they discovered certain patterns occured in predictable places. For instance, sounds like *reee woog woog* might follow *ara woog woog*. The sub-phrase *woog woog* may trigger the whale's memory for the passages that follow.

With all of these different interpretations, the father of humpback song research, Roger Payne, is the first to admit that we really don't know why whales sing or what their songs are about. We do, however, know that the study of whales is central to our finding ways to save them. We are also beginning to understand what environmental activist Michael

Bailey has been saying for years, "The whale is a marker for how well mankind is doing in our own quest for survival on this planet."

So it is not surprising that each winter and spring when the humpbacks migrate to Hawai'i from the frigid, krill-rich seas off Alaska, they attract scientists and tourists alike. After more than a century, Hawai'i is again headquarters for a whaling industry, but this time around the whale hunters use cameras and tape decks to photograph, study and enjoy the whales rather than harpoons to hunt them, as in the old days. Hawai'i's history is interlocked with nineteenth-century whalers and twentieth-century whale-watchers.

Behavioral psychologist Dr. Paul Forestell, whose research log book is reproduced below, summarized it when he said, "Right now we're all gathering as much information as we can about humpbacks — their feeding, breeding, fighting, singing, and of course, migration. I guess the bottom line for me is just two basic questions. First, what is a whale? And second, why do I care so much?"

Scientifically, researchers are making gains on Forestell's first question, and author-photographer Chris Newbert eloquently answers the second in his book of underwater experiences, *Within a Rainbowed Sea*:

"Floating there, I was in a trance, hypnotized not by any jewel, but by the singing of a massive Humpback Whale. It sounded close, so very close. But where was it? It seemed I could see forever down, and all around. At 45 to 50 feet in length and up to 90,000 pounds, this titanic mammal should have been easy to spot.

"Holding my breath, I slipped silently beneath the surface and allowed myself to glide downward. The further I descended, the louder became the haunting, sepulchral melody. Through my fins, up my legs, until my entire body actually vibrated, I could feel the resonance of this leviathan. I was so damned near! Yet there was not a thing to see in any direction except blue. Endless, brilliant, featureless blue. The sea around me was saturated with song, as if I were in a cathedral with a 45-ton pipe organ filling the air. I was enveloped in the spirit of this phantom whale, spellbound, with time suspended. I felt as if I were drawing energy directly from the sound waves, alive with this life force pulsing through the water, coursing through my body, then dispersing through an infinite sea.

"I could have kept going down. That was the easy part. Getting back up would have been another story. I never did see the whale, but it hardly matters, for his song is within me still."

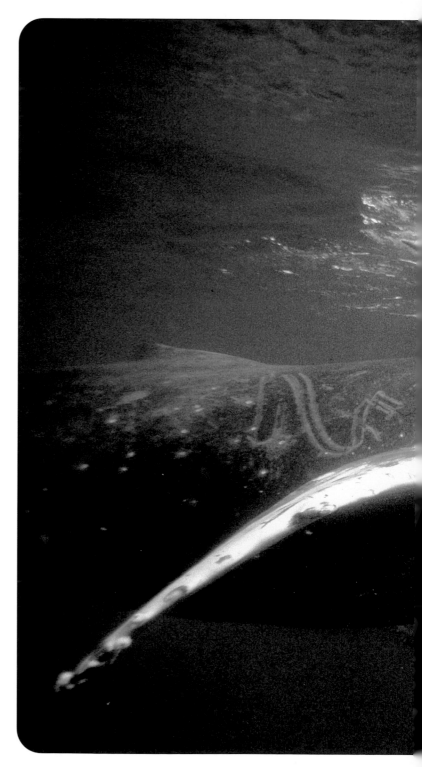

Right: Humpback mother and calf.

Photograph © 1989 by James Watt

141

About this Book

*I*n March 1986, the Macintosh Plus and LaserWriter were arriving in Apple dealerships across the land; Paul Brainerd launched PageMaker and coined the phrase "desktop publishing;" and an old friend, MacKinnon Simpson, called to ask if I'd help create a four page brochure for a Maui whaling museum.

I had just completed a book publishing project using traditional tools and methods. The good news was that these new books were winning major awards for excellence. The bad news arrived daily with the postman — unexpectedly high bills for typesetting, design, paste-up, color separations, stripping— the list seemed endless. And each bill we received reminded us of how dependent we were on these high priests of the craft.

The whaling museum brochure was a perfect way to try the new desktop technology, and so I went out the next day to buy a Mac Plus. On stray bits of paper, I calculated all the money, time and aggravation I would soon save by pioneering in this new desktop world.

Co-authors MacKinnon Simpson and Robert B. Goodman

Nothing worked out as I had planned, which I have come to understand is a *universal law* of which only I seemed ignorant..

I didn't really save any money because there were so many things to buy that were absolutely *essential* to creating that brochure on my desktop.

I did and I didn't save time, by which I mean that I did save on a task by task basis; but then spent the time I saved, and more, in making the job I was doing BETTER! So I really didn't save any time at all!

As to aggravation? Well, I did avoid aggravation with OTHER people, but replaced it with aggravation at my own ineptness. I discovered what I had long suspected: I am a computer idiot, a "techno-moron," in the words of a computer salesman I once knew. I would turn the Macintosh on and leave it running for days, fearful that if I shut it off, I couldn't get those little icons back on the screen where I had left them. My partner Simpson and I pooled the few things we knew about our Macs and watched our little brochure assignment turn into the national award-wining *WhaleSong*. How could that happen?

The simple and truthful answer is that Apple's advertising is correct. These tools gave us "the power to be our best," extraordinary power to create layouts and design pages, then to see them in seconds in 300 dots per inch (dpi) resolution. No more typesetters. No leaky Rapidograph pens. No huge costs whenever I saw a way to improve a layout or text block after it was ready for the printer. I was in control of my own storytelling again, and it was heaven!

This is not to say creating *WhaleSong* on our desktop was easy. It wasn't. Both Word 1.05 and Page-Maker 1.1 were young programs, and had to be coaxed to create text that at least mimicked real typesetting. Seeing early proof pages, Paul Brainerd said, "I never intended PageMaker to do *this*!"

The big question was Linotronic or LaserWriter? Should we use the Laser-Writer's 300 dot per inch output, or the 2,540 dpi output of Linotype's industry leading Linotronic L-300? I looked at test samples of *WhaleSong* in both versions and my eyes said that the LaserWriter's output looked really good. I mean, how many people use a jeweler's loupe to examine printed type?

WhaleSong arrived to rave reviews. Editor David Bunnell called it, "a landmark in American publishing." The New York Times featured it on page one. Apple sent a copy to every dealer in the country. Desktop trainers and computer buyers loved it. *WhaleSong* showed that this new technology could be used for more than just newsletters.

Within weeks of its introduction, *WhaleSong* was on its way to becoming a desktop publishing classic!

So, why a new edition? Because, quite frankly, I was hooked on the world of Macintosh. Everything about it was exciting. Everyone involved seemed to glow with enthusiasm. Just being part of it was intoxicating, and in its own way, an intensely loving experience. We were all *family*. Shy programmers and gregarious marketing execs all shared the same dream. There was room for everyone, including me, and I loved it. So *WhaleSong* was reborn, and this time created with the latest color technology, much of it light-years ahead of what we had used for the first edition.

My original Mac Plus still glowed happily, and had been joined by an SE, two SyQuest 45 megabyte removable cartridge drives, and an 80 megabyte Peripheral Land sealed drive that seemed more than adequate in capacity for almost any kind of image storage. I felt absolutely cocky about my setup until the decision was made to actually *DO* desktop color for the new *WhaleSong*.

Within days my world of hardware changed dramatically. First came a Mac II, which I soon discovered needed 8 megabytes of RAM to even begin handling its new tasks. Our first foray showed us how much data was being pushed through the Mac II's 68020, and we ordered a SiClone 3033 accelerator to bring us up to and beyond Mac IIx standards.

Then I began learning about the differences in color monitors and chose Radius with their 24/32 bit card. Screen redraws are slow in 24 bit. Again, Radius had the product, a bargain price RISC-based board called QuickColor which sped everything up from three to six times. Before long we had Radius monitors everywhere. They are *that* good! We added FPD's for the Plus and SE, and a gray scale TPD for a second Mac II.

Following our earlier efforts we had settled on the HP ScanJet Plus for gray scale scanning.

Color Scanning? Computer magazines were filled with comparative tests, most of which looked washed out and, to be frank, horrible. Color scanners seemed to vie with each other for muddiness and lack of contrast. I had this wild idea that full professional color scanning had already arrived, all evidence to the contrary notwithstanding!

Faced with choosing a color scanner, I saw two clear paths and chose both. As a photojournalist I had learned that 35mm could easily be enlarged to 40x60 inches and look great. So it was natural for me to decide on the Barneyscan V3, which is a maturing system and a superb 35mm scanner.

Art also comes as large transparencies, or flats. To scan these we chose Sharp's magnificent JX-450, an 11x17 inch flatbed 300 dpi color scanner. Just as we were readying this new *WhaleSong* for press, Sharp's 600 dpi color scanner became available, and we rushed to use it for images in our companion volume.

Color scanning required both color retouching software and separation routines for the heretofore difficult task of turning the RGB scan into the four colors needed by the printer. For both tasks, Adobe's new Photoshop, written by programmer Tom Knoll, was, even in its Alpha form, a brilliant performer. It was miraculous to see color retouching, cloning, anti-aliasing, masking, etc. on the Radius monitor — tasks, always before, left to the million dollar systems.

Desktop color demands memory—the reliable, fast and sturdy 45 megabyte SyQuest removable cartridge drives enhanced by PLI saved us. Some of our scans were 18 megabytes in size! For these, the 600 megabyte PLI Infinity magneto optical worked wonders.

We depended on other powerful programs like Illustrator 88, Streamline, Broderbund's new Type-Styler, and PageMaker's 3.02 Color Extension,and of course, Freehand.

We networked via Farallon's PhoneNET Connectors, StarController, & incredible Timbuktu/Remote.

Then there were specialty programs such as The Night Watch and Tops, and *everything* CE software made, programs you find that you simply can't do without. In the same category were the peripheral devices sold by Kensington. I call them the "little graces" because life with them was genuinely better.

Color proofing was primarily done on the industry leading QMS ColorScript 100. We also worked with Hewlett Packard's PaintJet and Sharp's full 11x17 inch color inkjet printers. To nail down color selections we leaned on Pantone's new electronic PMS color system. All black and white laser printing was done on the QMS 810.

We needed more elegant type for the new edition of *WhaleSong* and Stone Serif from Adobe worked perfectly. New calligraphy and chapter headings were hand-created by Adobe designer Robert Slimbach to complement the Sumner Stone typeface.

When it came down to film, everything was output to the new RIP3 Linotronic L-300, which day after trouble-free day cranked out flawless pages for our printer, Dynagraphics in Portland, Oregon. That film was color proofed for the printer with 3M Color Keys created using either a nuARC or Burgess Triple Spectrum printer. The book that resulted is in your hands, and, of course the full story cannot be told on these two pages. The OCR rescue we performed with TextPert; the 24 hour a day <u>anywhere</u> work capability provided by our Colby Walkmac; the promotional pizazz that came with Weyerhaeuser's new electro-imaging paper, First Choice, all added to our pleasure in assembling this new edition of *WhaleSong*. That full story is told in a 32-page companion volume, *Creating a Macintosh Classic — The Story of WhaleSong.*

Robert B. Goodman

The Lahaina
Whaling Museum

The story behind the Lahaina Whaling Museum is the story of one man's urge to collect and to share.

Rick Ralston, founder of Crazy Shirts, is a successful Island businessman. And, far more than that, he is an artist, connoiseur, consummate perfectionist, eclectic collector and a guardian of the past. A number of historic homes in Hawai'i facing the "progress" of imminent demolition owe their preservation and restoration to Ralston. Today, these same homes are filled with period antiques, and Ralston's Crazy Shirts factory headquarters and shops are decorated with other fruits of his collecting — cigar store Indians, pressed-steel toys, jukeboxes and nickleodeons, and Hawaiiana. One Crazy Shirts shop on Kaua'i, in 1890 a plantation General Store, still sells chilled Cokes — in green glass bottles — for a nickel. (They cost him 50¢!)

During Ralston's first visit to Lahaina in 1964, he fell totally in love with the historic town and its century-oldwhaling seaport atmosphere. It was then that he began collecting whaling artifacts from the 1800s — a collection assembled over the next twenty years both in Hawai'i and on trips back to the old Yankee whaling centers of Mystic, Nantucket,and New Bedford. The growing collection found its way into displays in Lahaina, until sheer numbers mandated a permanent home. Ralston then contacted conservator Mildred Valentine and architect Robert Herlinger, and charged them with designing a whaling and maritime museum for Lahaina's Front Street. The result, the Lahaina Whaling Museum, is free to the public, and celebrates more than a half-century of Maui's past. Right on the ocean, it faces Lahaina Roads where the old whaleships anchored, and is just a few doors down from the site of the notorious, uproarious "Whale Fluke's Inn," where merriment abounded —both downstairs and up.

Created under commission from Lahaina Whaling Museum, *WhaleSong* is dedicated to sharing the story of whales in Hawai'i's past, present and future.

Top: *Rick Ralston, creator of the Museum.*
Bottom: *A popular attraction for photographers ("Stand right there next to him, Edna, and hold onto his harpoon!"), Elmo Gates welcomes visitors to the picturesque Lahaina Whaling Museum at 865 Front Street. Harpooneer Gates was carved by famed Maui sculptor, Reems Mitchell.*

Glossary

aft: the back, or stern, of boat or ship.

ambergris: valuable,waxy clump of matter found in large intestines of some sperm whales. Used as perfume fixative. Prices in mid-1800s ranged to $15/oz.

baleen: fringed filters in mouths of baleen whales. Used for corset stays,buggy whips, and other applications requiring flexibility. Holds its shape when heated and bent. See whalebone.

baleen whales: *(Mysticeti)* filter-feeder whales, such as the right, bowhead and humpback.

bark: a ship with three masts, short for barkentine.

barrel: a whalers' unit of measurement equalling 31.5 gallons. See also casks.

Bible leaves: thin-sliced blubber still attached to the outer skin of the whale.

blanket piece: large strip of blubber peeled off the whale and brought on deck for cutting.

blubber: the thick layer of fat, serving as insulation and flotation, on a whale's body. The whalers boiled it for oil.

blubber hook: the large iron hook, attached by block and tackle to a mast, used to peel blubber from whale.

blubber room: area belowdecks where blubber was cut into progressively smaller pieces for melting.

boatsteerer: another name for the harpooneer, because after planting the harpoon(s), he would switch places with the mate and steer the boat.

bodkin: a small pointed needle, often carved of ivory or wood, used to poke holes in cloth to draw thread through.

bow: the front of a boat or ship.

bowhead whale: a large baleen whale rich in oil and whalebone found in Arctic waters.

breach: for a whale to leap clear, or almost clear, of the water.

brig: a two-masted ship

brigantine: a two-masted ship with square-rigged front and fore-and-aft rear.

brogans: high-top shoes with only two lace-holes for quick removal. Except in coldest weather, the whalers would take off their shoes before getting into the whaleboats so as not to scare off the whales, whose hearing was apparently better than their sense of smell.

bull: a fully-grown male whale.

busk: a flexible corset stay usually made commercially of baleen. These were a favorite item for the whalers to scrimshaw and, in the absence of baleen, they would occasionally use panbone.

caraboose: a brick-and-mortar trough beneath the tryworks, which was filled with sea water to insulate the wooden decks from the heat of the fires. Also called duck-ponds.

case: cavity in a sperm whale's nose holding the waxy spermaceti, which was bailed-out by hand.

cask: barrels, usually oak, to store oil. The term barrel itself was a unit of measurement equalling 31.5 gallons. Casks were of different sizes to fit better in the hold, and usually contained 5 to 15 barrels each (150 to 472 gallons).

center-board: a tempoary keel dropped through a slot in the whaleboat's floor and needed for stability when the sail was up. Still used on small sailboats.

chandler: a ship-supply dealer.

chock: groove in the whaleboat's bow through which the whaleline ran.

chock-pin: slender wooden pin slipped into the chock to keep the whaleline in place. It was the harpooneer's job to insert this pin, and he would often carve miniatures of it out of ivory to stick in his hat as a badge of honor and mark him as a harpooneer.

clumsy cleat: a notch cut into bow of the whaleboat where harpooneer wedged his leg to steady himself. For a right-hander, clumsy cleat was cut for his left leg, and vice-versa if he was left-handed.

cooper: the cask-maker, assembled casks up on deck as needed for the oil.

crimp: see shipping agent.

crisps: blubber after oil was boiled out. Used to feed try-works fires and occasionally eaten as a deep-fried snack.

cross-trees: the horizontal masts on a square-rigger.

crow's nest: the station high on mast where a lookout stood. See also hoops.

cutting-in: slicing blubber off whale.

cutting stage: a hinged platform lowered over whale's carcass for cutting-in.

davits: supports to which whaleboat was hooked to raise and lower it.

distress flag: A whaleship in trouble would fly its flag upside-down.

ditty-bag: a cloth bag with a sailor's small personal belongings.

double-ended: a boat pointed on both ends to be rowed backwards and forwards equally well. Whaleboats and canoes are both double-ended craft.

drogue: a wood float attached to the harpoon to keep a whale from diving easily and tire him out. Sometimes a cask was used by early land whalers.

duck-ponds: See caraboose.

fan: spout of a whale. See spout.

fathom: a measure of six feet.

fid: long pointed needle-like tool of wood or ivory used to separate rope strands for splicing.

flensing: stripping blubber off whale.

flukes: horizontal tail of the whale used for propulsion and as a weapon. Up to 20' across.

flurry: the whale's death throes in which he would thrash about in the water. Also called flutters.

flutters: see flurry.

forecastle, or fo'c's'le: small room in the bow of the ship, one deck down, where the crew lived.

gam: meeting between two whaleships at sea. Whalers would visit each other's ships and exchange news from home, books and whaling information.

grog: a mixture of rum and water adored by sailors and abhorred by missionaries.

grounds: areas in ocean where whales would congregate, as the Japan Grounds.

gunwale: rim along the sides of a ship or boat, pronounced 'gunnel.'

hardtack: thick hard crackers.

harpoon: barbed spear used to attach the whale to the whaleboat.

harpooneer: crew member designated to harpoon the whale, also boatsteerer.

herd: name of a group of sperm whales. Other species are called pods.

hermaphrodite brig: three-masted ship, with square-rigged mainmast and sloop rigging on the fore and aft masts.

hold: space in a ship's hull for cargo; in a whaler for casks of oil.

hoops: iron rings above highest crosstrees, as a safety guard for the lookouts.

hull: framework of a ship.

iron: another name for harpoon.

jib rig: a triangular sail stretching forward from the mast.

krill: small marine organisms on which baleen whales feed.

lance: slender pointed spear used to pierce the whale's heart or lungs.

lantern keg: small sealed survival kit kept in a whaleboat containing a lantern, candles, matches, tobacco and hardtack.

larboard: left, or port.

lay: a percentage of net voyage profits. Whalers were not salaried but were paid on commission.

line tub: tub used to hold about 300 fathoms (1800') of carefully-coiled line.

lobtail: thrashing of a whale's flukes against the whaleboat.

loggerhead: wooden post around which the whaleline was wrapped and spun as it payed out.

mainmast: tallest mast on a ship.

mating: two whaleships hunting together and evenly dividing their catch.

mizzenmast: a ships rear mast.

Mocha Dick: legendary (but real) sperm whale — named after the Mocha Islands off Chile — blamed for attacking and sinking the *Essex* in 1820, as well as destroying many whaleboats and their crews. Mocha Dick was the basis for Herman Melville's novel, *Moby Dick*.

monkey rope: safety line to keep men from falling off the cutting-stage.

Nantucket Sleigh Ride: a tow in a boat hooked to a fast-swimming whale.

nipper: piece of canvas or leather used to protect hands holding line paying out.

octant: instrument of navigation used to measure ship's position.

pan-bone: sperm whale's lower jaw.

piggin: small wooden bucket with one long stave as handle, for bailing boat.

pike: wooden-handled tool used to manuver large pieces of blubber.

plum duff: a pudding-like dessert delicacy of molasses, raisins and sugar occasionally containing, as an added treat, splinters from the molasses barrel.

pod: school of whales (except sperms, which were called a herd).

point: unusual unit used to measure direction, equalling 1/32 of a circle. With ship as center, four quadrants were dead ahead, dead astern, starboard beam (r) and larboard beam (l). Each was divided into eight points, so a whale might be "three points off starboard."

port: left, also called larboard.

port-painted: an early form of camouflage. An unarmed or lightly-armed ship was painted to look as if she had gunports for cannons along both sides to frighten off pirates or natives.

red flag: the blooded spout of a mortally wounded whale.

run: for a harpooned whale to take off along the surface, as opposed to sound.

scrimshander: one who scrimshaws.

sea chest: a chest in the forecastle, with a sailor's extra clothing and gear.

sextant: navigational instrument used for determining ship's position.

sheathing: overlapping copper plates nailed over the ship's bottom to protect against seaworms.

shipping agent: recruiters for sailors. Many were unscrupulous and used chicanery, alcohol, sex and often force to fill the forecastle. The lowest of the low were called 'crimps' and at least one, San Francisco's notorious Miss Piggot, occasionally shipped corpses—carried aboard and assumed to be dead drunk instead of vice-versa.

shooks: unassembled, pre-cut casks put together as needed by the cooper. Pronounced 'shukes.'

shrouds: rigging running from the masts to the sides of the ship.

sloop: small one-masted vessel with fore and aft sails.

slop chest: the ship's store, offering clothing, tobacco and other small items, often at exorbitant prices.

slow helm: sluggish response to steering inputs. A whaleship's shape gave it a slow helm.

sound: for the harpooned whale to dive deep rather than run across the surface.

spade: sharp, flat-bladed tool used to cut the blubber into blanket pieces.

spermaceti: waxy substance found in the sperm whale's case. It is liquid at body temperature and solidifies as it cools Early whalers thought it was the reproductive fluid (hence "sperm" whale).

spout: vapor emitted from the whale's nostril(s) after a dive. Each species has a distinctive, recognizable, spout shape.

spy-hop: whale raising the head vertically out of the water to see.

square-rig: sails mounted at right angles to the ship.

starboard: ship's right side.

starn all! the mate's command to row away from a just-harpooned whale.

stave: one of the pieces of curved wood in the side of a barrel.

steerage: belowdecks amid-ship where specialists (harpooneers, cooper) lived.

steering oar: long stern oar of a whaleboat by which the mate or boatsteerer manuvered.

stern: the rear of a ship or boat.

stove in: crushed by a whale's tail, as in a 'stove boat.'

swift: a complicated whalebone and ivory scrimshaw creation that expanded or contracted around a center post. It was used for winding yarn, and was usually made by one of the officers.

thar she blows: the lookout's cry that he has seen a whale spouting.

thwart: seat in a boat.

toggle iron: harpoon with swiveling head, which locked it in place.

toothed whales: *(Odontoceti)* whales with teeth, such as the sperms, narwhals and porpoises.

trying out: process of boiling the whale blubber into oil.

try-pot: large cast-iron pot of about 250 gallon capacity used to boil blubber.

tryworks: brick-framed stove which enclosed the try-pots on the deck of a whaleship. The fires to boil the oil were started with wood, then fed with crisps.

waif: small flag on a wooden pole stuck into the whale to mark it if the whaleboat had to leave.

whalebone: whaler's term for the flexible baleen, which was not actually bone, but keratin.

Index

A
Acushnet (whaler), 91
Alabama (Confederate warship), 107
Algonquin Indian Nation, 16, 79
Allen, E.S. 102
Allen, Captain Joseph, 98
American Revolution, 27
Antarctica, 27, 31
Ashley, Clifford, 55
Awashonks (whaler), 113
B
Bailey, Michael, 121, 122, 139
Balcom, Lowell LeRoy, 25, 26, 89
Balena (whaler), 34
Barber, Captain Albert, 106
Barker, Captain Frederick, 112
Basques, 16
Bay of Fundy, Maine, 49
Beaver (whaler), 33
Belcher's Bay, Alaska, 113
Benjamin Tucker (whaler), 106
Bering Strait, 103
Beston, Henry, 1
Bingham, Hiram, 39
Brewer, Charles, 99
Brewer, C. (company) 99
Brewster (whaler), 29
Buddington, Captain J.W., 20
Burgess, George, 98
Burke, Edmund, 26
Burns, Henry, 103
C
California Gold Rush, 103, 107
Cape Horn, 27, 30, 31, 32, 34
Cape of Good Hope, 31
Cape Verde Islands, 68, 79
Castle, Samuel Northrup, 44, 99
Castle & Cooke, 99
Chamberlain, Daniel, 39, 42
Charles and Henry (whaler), 91
Charles W. Morgan (whaler), 29
Charleston, S.C., 107
Cheever, Rev., 96
Children of the Light (book), 102
Choris, Louis, 42
Civil War, see War between the States
Clara Bell (whaler) 73, 113
Clark, Helen (Jernegan), 49
Clinton, Sir Henry, 27
Comet (whaler), 110
Cook, Captain James, 34, 38, 41
Cook, Captain John, 117
Cooke, Amos Starr, 44, 99
Cooper, Captain Mercator, 109
Cox, Captain William H., 95
D
Daniel (whaler), 98
Davies, Theo H., 102
Davies, Theo H, (company) 102
Davis, William M., 80
Dibble, Sheldon, 91, 96
Dowden, Captain James, 113
Drake's Passage, 34
Driftnetting, 119, 124, 125
E
Earthtrust, 119, 121-5, 129
Edgartown, Martha's Vineyard, 49
Electrolyte Marine Salts Company, 49
Emerald (whaler), 103
Emerson, N.B., 105
Emilia (whaler), 27, 31, 33, 34
Emily Morgan (whaler), 49
Emmert, Paul, 98
Equator (whaler), 34
Eskimos, 16, 112
Essex (whaler), 83
Essex (U.S. frigate), 33

Essex, Massachusetts, 117
Ewer, Captain Prince W., 49
F
Falkland Islands, 27
Ferguson, William, 55
Ferrari, Mark & Deborah Glockner, 137, 138
Figurehead, 2
First Company, 39, 42, 44
Fisher, Captain Charles, 60
Fisher, Charles, 49
Forestell, Paul, 139
Foyn, Captain Svend, 117
G
Galapagos Islands, 91
Greener's gun, 84-5
Gregg, David L., 107
Guinee, Linda, 139
Gurrick, James, 115
H
Hackfeld, H., 99
Hackler, Rhoda E.A., 95
Hale Piula, 97
Hector (whaler), 33
Herman, Dr. Louis, 138
History of Nantucket, 20
Holman, Dr. Thomas, 42
Holt, John Dominis, 102
Honolulu Iron Works, 98
Howland, Captain, 56
Humphrey, the Wayward Whale, 138
Hunnewell, James, 99
Hussey, Captain Christopher, 23
J
James Bay (ship), 121, 122
Japan (whaler), 112
Japan, 109
Japan Whaling Grounds, 34, 38, 109
Jefferson, Thomas, 28
Jernegan, Captain Jared, 49
Jernegan, Laura, 46, 47-9
Jernegan, Prescott, 49
John Howland (whaler), 49
John Palmer (whaler), 99
Judd, Gerrit, 44
K
Kamamalu (wife of Kamehameha II), 44
Kamehameha I (the Great), 38, 42, 44
Kamehameha II (Liholiho), 42, 44
Kamehameha III, 102
Kanakas, 29, 100-1
Kanaloa, Hawaiian God, 9, 16, 43
Kathleen (whaler), 55, 56
Kealakekua Bay. Hawaii, 40
Kewalo Basin Marine Mammal Lab, 138
Key, Francis Scott, 33
Kimball family, 64
King James I, 16
Kohala (whaler), 112
Kutusoff (whaler), 40, 94-5
L
L'Aigle (whaler), 44
LaBudde, Sam, 125
Lahaina, Maui, 97-8, 115, 119
Lahainaluna Seminary, 44, 97
Lancing (ship), 118
Lay (division of profits), 29, 95
Lei niho palaoa, 16, 42, 43
Liholiho, (see Kamehameha II)
Lindbergh, Charles A., 37
Logbook, 29, 73-7, 139
Loomis, Elisha, 44
Lucy Ann (whaler), 91
M
Ma'alea Bay, Maui, 117
Macy, Obed, 20
Magellan, Ferdinand, 37
Manhattan (whaler), 108-9
Margaret (whaler), 20-1
Marin, Don, 42
Maro (whaler), 98
Mars (whaler), 87
Martha's Vineyard, 49
Mayflower Pilgrim Colony, 16, 20
Melville, Herman, 25, 41, 80, 86, 91, 128
Moby Dick, 25, 41, 80, 83
Monticello (whaler), 87, 113
Morgan, C.W., 49
Morison, Samuel Eliot, 41

N
Newbert, Chris, 139
Newfoundland, 23
Nordhoff, Charles, 51, 91, 103
North America (whaler), 120
Nu'uanu Valley, 98
Nye's Sperm Oil, 98
O
Obookiah, Henry (Opukahaia), 39, 42
Octant, 72
Ohana Kai (ship), 122
P
Pacific Commercial Advertiser, 113, 115
Paddock, Ichabod, 20
Panorama, 40-1, 96-7
Parker, John Palmer, 42
Parker Ranch, 102
Payne, Katherine & Roger, 138-9
Peirce, Captain A.W., 104-5
Peirce, Sarah (Bright), 105
Perry, Commodore Matthew, 109
Petroleum, 107
"Philippines, My Phillipines" (song), 49
Phyllis Cormack (ship), 121
Port-painted, 95
Portland, Maine, 117
Progress (whaler), 113
Purrington, Caleb, 40, 41, 97
R
Raleigh, Charles S., 28, 29
Rebecca (whaler), 33
Richards, Rev. William, 44, 99
"Rollin' Down to Old Mowee"(song) 69
Roman (whaler), 49, 112
Rotch, Captain, 70
Royal Charter of 1620, 16
Roys, Captain, 103
Rurik (Russian Navy), 42
Russell, Benjamin, 40-1, 94-5, 96-7
S
Sandwich, Earl of, 38
Scammon, Charles M., 84
Scrimshaw, 25, 29, 50-67
Sea Dragon (boat), 121
Shenandoah (Confederate warship), 107
Silva, Captain, 112
Simpson, Sir George, 99
Sovreign of the Seas (clipper), 37
Spencer, Captain Thomas, 106
Starbuck, Captain Valentine, 44
Stangenwald, Hugo, 106
Stewart, Rev. Charles S., 32
Stone Fleet, 107
Sugar, 107
Sumter, Fort, 107
Sumter (Confederate warship), 107
Superior (whaler), 103
T
Taipi (tribe), 91
Takahashi, Caroline, 123
Tamerlane (whaler), 101
Temple, Lewis, 16
Thames, (whaler), 32
Thaddeus, 42, 44
Thurston, Asa, 44
Triumph, 39
Triton (whaler), 106
Typee, 80
U
United States (warship), 91
V
Viola (whaler), 92-3
von Kutzebue, Otto, 42
W
Wampanoag tribe, 20, 79
War between the States, 33
War of 1812, 33
Washington (whaler), 33
Whalers' Riot, 103
Whitney, Samuel, 44
Whelden, Mrs. Alexander, 49
White, Don, 122, 128
Whitecar, William, 55
Williams, Captain Thomas, 113
Wives, whaling, 34, 46, 49
Y
Young, John (Old), 42
Young, Olivia, 123

ACKNOWLEDGEMENTS

Many people offered their help during the creation of this second edition of *WhaleSong,* and hopefully we have remembered them all.

First and foremost, our thanks to **Rick Ralston** and **Kim Scoggins** at Crazy Shirts for their support and wonderful sense of humor as this project has unfolded.

And our heartfelt aloha to our printers, Char & Byron Liske and their superb staff at Dynagraphics.

Our thanks also to **Tony Hodges,** for his endless encouragement and insight.

To the many, many people in the computer industry who have supported this project and shared our dreams. In particular, we would like to warmly thank at — **Adobe:** Liz Bond, Gail Blumberg, Steve Guttman, Russell Brown, and Russ Fujioka; **Aldus:** Vickie Farmer; **Apple:** Peter Lycurgus, Alan Hallberg, and Deborah Turner; **Barneyscan:** Tom Moore, Paul Buxbaum, Steve Schaffran, and Howard Barney; **Belknap Productions:** Jodi and Buzz Belknap, Scott Matsushige, Kelly Minato, Steve Nickerson, and Kym L. Miller; **Beyond Words Publishing** in Hillsboro, OR: Richard and Cyndi Cohn; **Broderbund Software:** Larry Berkin, Christopher Allen, Harry Wilker, and Nanci Buck; **David Bunnel; Colby Systems:** Chuck and Karen Colby; **Cole Gilburne Fund:** David Cole, Miles Gilburne, and Nat Goldhaber; **Connecting Point:** Mike Klein and staff; **C.T.A. TextPert:** Craig Moody; **Federal Express:** Cliff Deeds; **Field Enterprises:** Terry, Debby, and Mark Borton; **John S. Harcourt; Hewlett Packard:** Naomi Overton and Jeri Peterson; **Bree James; Kensington:** Pam Miller, Rosie McClellan, and Susan Lefkowitz; **Ken Kimura; Linotype:** Rod Bush, and Pat Greatzer; **Joel Lovingfoss; Lithocolor:** Gordon Hess and staff; **MacWEEK:** Cyndi Ahart and Michael Tchong; **Pairs Software:** David Rice and Mark Olmstead; **Pantone:** Candice Eagle, Richard Hebert, Lisa Herbert, Jay di Sibour; **Peripheral Land:** Tad Shelby, Frank Jaramillo; **Publish Magazine:** Steven Jones; **QMS Corporation:** Rick Armstrong & Ann Strople; **Radius:** Mike Boich, Ed Colligan, Steve Holtzman, Ginny Merrifield, Jeannie Lyle, and Carole Dyce; **Rick Carroll & Associates:** Rick Carroll; **Seybold, Inc.:** Jonathan Seybold; **Sharp:** Duane Miller, Bill Robinson, Tom Bongiorno, and Mark Albanese; **SiClone:** Stuart Russell, Kay Lemon; **Software Architects:** Carl Nelson, and Bob Zollo; **SyQuest:** Sayed Iftikar, Boris Zbicki, and Craig Cockrum; **Weyerhaeuser Paper Company:** Fred Dempsey and Alan T. Winslow.

Our thanks and warmest Aloha to our friends in the travel industry: Randy Ko and Patty Clark at **United Air Lines;** Virginia Terwilliger, Dick Smith, and Edie Kianfor at **United Vacations;** Milton Goto at **Aloha Airlines;** Peter Dudgeon at **Aloha Island Air;** Tom Morrish, Tom Nieman, and Pete Sanborn at **Village Resorts;** Eugene Cotter, at the **Hawaii Visitors Bureau,** Bill Cook at the **State of Hawaii DBED,** and Bill Bass at **HTDC.**

SPECIAL EDITORIAL CONTRIBUTIONS

Richard Ellis whose paintings appear on pages 22-23, 24 is world reknowned

for his best selling books on whales, dolphins, and sharks. Since 1980, he has been a voting member of the U.S. Delegation to the International Whaling Commission.

Deborah A. Glockner-Ferrari and **Mark J. Ferrari** are a whale research team who spend most of each year studying the humpback in Hawaiian waters. Her photograph on page 138 was taken under federal permit granted by the NMFS & State permit by the State of Hawaii, Department of Land and Natural Resources. The Ferraris can be reached at the Center For Whale Studies, P.O. Box 1539, Lahaina, Hawaii 96767-1539.

Steven Michael Gardner, whose painting graces pages 12-13, granted reproduction rights as a contribution to Earthtrust. One of America's leading environmental artists, Gardner's images have been widely published and are also available in posters and note cards. He can be reached at Gardner Graphics, 4784 Andalusia Ave., San Diego, CA 92117.

Herb Kawainui Kane whose painting appears on pages 14-15, is Hawai'i's artist/historian. Kane's paintings are in the permanent collections of the State Foundation on Culture and the Arts, the National Park Service, and The National Geographic Society. Kane has designed six U.S. postage stamps. He resides in South Kona, Hawaii where he tends his young plantation of gourmet avocados.

Christopher Newbert, whose photographs are on pages 10-11, 130-131, 135, and the cover, is without equal as an underwater photographer. His book, *Within a Rainbowed Sea,* published by Beyond Words Publishing Company, is the all time best selling underwater book.

Schim Schimmel, whose painting appears on page eight is a concerned environmentalist whose imaginative works have attracted the attention of collectors worldwide. This whale painting, also a poster, is one of two that Schim created to benefit Earthtrust. He can be reached through his gallery, Collector's Editions Inc, Suite D, Canoga Park, CA 91304.

Robert Slimbach created the roman style and brush calligraphy for this book. Mr. Slimbach has a worldwide reputation for type design, including the honor of having created typefaces for the ITC library. He currently works at Adobe Systems in Mountain View, California.

James D. Watt, whose photographs appear on pages 126-127, 128, 132-133, 134, 136-137, & 140-141 is one of the most published marine mammal photographers in the world. His company, Ocean Editions, specializes in marine mammal reproductions, and is located at P.O. Box 598, Kealakekua, HI 96750.

ENVIRONMENTAL RESEARCH

Don and Susan White, and **Michael Bailey** of Earthtrust at 2500 Pali Highway, Honolulu, HI 96817.

Katharine Payne and **Linda Guinee,** of Cornell University's Laboratory of Ornithology, and Long Term Research Institute, Lincoln, Mass., respectively.